Making Sense

Understanding, as Descartes, Locke and Kant all insisted, is the primary 'faculty' of the mind; yet our modern sciences have been slow to advance a clear and testable account of what it means to understand, of children's acquisition of this concept and, in particular, how children come to ascribe understanding to themselves and others. By drawing together developmental and philosophical theories, this book provides a systematic account of children's concept of understanding and places understanding at the heart of children's 'theory of mind'. Children's subjective awareness of their own minds, of what they think, depends on learning a language for ascribing mental states to themselves and others. This book will appeal to researchers in developmental psychology, cognitive science, education and philosophy who are interested in the cognitive and emotional development of children and in the more basic question of what it means to have a mind.

David R. Olson is University Professor Emeritus at the Ontario Institute for Studies in Education at the University of Toronto, Canada. He has authored more than 300 articles and 20 books, including *The World on Paper* (Cambridge, 1994), *Psychological Theory and Educational Reform: How School Remakes Mind and Society* (Cambridge, 2004) and *The Mind on Paper* (Cambridge, 2016). His research focuses on children's developing consciousness of their own and others' mental states and on the role that language and literacy play in this development.

T0372653

Making Sense

What It Means to Understand

DAVID R. OLSON

University of Toronto

CAMBRIDGE
UNIVERSITY PRESS

Shaftesbury Road, Cambridge CB2 8EA, United Kingdom

One Liberty Plaza, 20th Floor, New York, NY 10006, USA

477 Williamstown Road, Port Melbourne, VIC 3207, Australia

314–321, 3rd Floor, Plot 3, Splendor Forum, Jasola District Centre, New Delhi – 110025, India

103 Penang Road, #05–06/07, Visioncrest Commercial, Singapore 238467

Cambridge University Press is part of Cambridge University Press & Assessment, a department of the University of Cambridge.

We share the University's mission to contribute to society through the pursuit of education, learning and research at the highest international levels of excellence.

www.cambridge.org
Information on this title: www.cambridge.org/9781009073523

DOI: 10.1017/9781009064569

First published 2022
First paperback edition 2024

A catalogue record for this publication is available from the British Library

Library of Congress Cataloging-in-Publication data
Names: Olson, David R., 1935– author.
Title: Making sense : what it means to understand / David R. Olson.
Description: 1 Edition. | New York, NY ; Cambridge : Cambridge University Press, 2022. | Includes bibliographical references and index.
Identifiers: LCCN 2021054357 | ISBN 9781316513330 (hardback) | ISBN 9781009073523 (paperback) | ISBN 9781009064569 (epub)
Subjects: LCSH: Comprehension. | Cognitive learning. | BISAC: PSYCHOLOGY / Developmental / General
Classification: LCC BF325 .O57 2022 | DDC 370.15/23–dc23/eng/20211230
LC record available at https://lccn.loc.gov/2021054357

ISBN   978-1-316-51333-0   Hardback
ISBN   978-1-009-07352-3   Paperback

Dedicated to Christopher Olsen, Lynd Forguson and
Joseph Heath

Contents

13 Understanding in Everyday Life   149

14 Ascriptivism and Cognitive Development   159

    References   181
    Index   193

Figures

Tables

Preface

This book reveals some of the uses and limitations of the extended isolation imposed by the COVID virus. It provided vast stretches of unscripted time but limited access to valued resources in the form of both colleagues, who normally provide a needed check on exuberance, and the resource materials available in an easily accessible reference library.

I dedicate the book to three philosophical colleagues who, over a span of many years, helped me to find the common ground between the philosophy of mind and the experimental developmental study of the mind: Christopher Olsen, with whom I co-taught a course for many years on the Cognitive Processes in Education, where we attempted to link the philosophy of Fodor, Chomsky, Dennett, and Searle to the psychological theories of Piaget, Vygotsky, and Bruner; Lynd Forguson, who urged me to read F. H. Bradley, P. Grice, and Donald Davidson and who enriched our research program by insisting that words and sentences should be seen as speech acts, things that speakers do and that they are responsible for; and Joseph Heath, who, through his own writings and through our discussions of Sellars, Rorty, and Brandom, convinced me that my Vygotskian views had much in common with, and could benefit from, the "linguistic turn" in philosophy.

In 1989, I tackled the topic explored in this book in a paper entitled "Making up your mind." It was my presidential address to the Canadian Psychological Association. I described a series of stages through which children pass as their cognitive processing resources increase, from perception to concepts to concepts about concepts, to show that "people are not born believers – they become believers." In rereading that paper today, I find that I agree with the general claim but address it in an entirely new way. Rather than the reorganization of private cognitive structures or "mental representations," I explain development in terms of the acquisition of mentalistic words such as "think" and "understand" and their uses in a publicly shared language. This has allowed me to address the gap between an objective account of cognitive development and the subjective experiences of the children themselves. But I hold true to the original aspiration, explaining mental life without simply denying it altogether or assuming it to be nature's gift. Rather, the mind is a product of language and education.

I am grateful to Janet Astington, Manuela Ungureanu, and Joseph Heath for their helpful comments on this volume and to my editor at Cambridge University Press, Janka Romero, who, with the help of anonymous readers, recommended the revisions that helped to turn the book from an inquiry into something resembling a theory.

1   An Introduction to the Puzzles of Understanding

> The knowledge of every understanding, or at least of the human understanding, must be by means of concepts, not intuitive, but discursive.
>
> —Kant, *Critique of Pure Reason*

When our daughter Joan was little more than a year old, on a whim I said to her, "Joanie, go get your shoes." To that point, she had never said a word or given any indication of understanding language, so my request was clearly unrealistic. Yet she looked at me briefly, wheeled around, and disappeared down the hallway. Moments later, she returned, shoes in hand and a smile on her face that expressed a pride matched only by that felt by her astonished father. She understood!

But what happened? What is understanding? John Locke's (1689) *An Essay Concerning Human Understanding* was among the first of a long list of attempts to explain understanding, work continued by such luminaries as Hume, Spinoza, Kant, and Husserl. In the twentieth century, inspired in part by Wittgenstein, the study of understanding shifted from mental processes to linguistic analysis, from mental states to language about those states.

Psychologists ordinarily take little interest in such philosophical or linguistic analyses, preferring to begin with observations of what subjects do under various conditions. They attempt to explain behavior without preconceptions. They tell stories, ask questions, and invent puzzles that seem to require understanding and, based on observations of the subject's performance, attribute mental representations and mental operations to them. Indeed, psychologists take it as odd that philosophers bother to analyze such vague and abstract notions as belief and understanding. They prefer to examine what subjects do, not investigate the properties of the word that appears to merely label the process: as if one could learn about horses by consulting a dictionary rather than visiting a farmyard.

Developmental psychology holds some promise of explaining what it means to understand by capturing young children's first understanding of language and later their learning the concept of understanding. By examining young children's understanding, it may be possible to throw light on the emergence of mental states in general. Experimental research on children's concepts often crosses the disciplinary boundaries between psychological, philosophical, and linguistic analysis. Boundary crossing is always hazardous.

Understanding would seem to be the most commonplace of all forms of experience. It is seeing what is going on, what is happening, putting two and two together, and reaching agreements. And we have all had the experience of understanding as insight, the dramatic grasping of the significance of an experience or the meaning of a story. We understand the feelings of others, and we know how distressing it is to realize when no one understands us. We understand or at least try to understand what we read. Some even know of the "fourfold meanings of scripture" – the literal, the allegorical, the metaphorical and the anagogical – and we know how to understand a variety of specialized forms of literature. If we want to know more, we can consult a dictionary that will inform us that to understand is to "grasp the meaning." So what's the problem?

The problem, as I hope to show, is that our certainties about understanding may be somewhat illusory, an illusion that leads us to think we understand when we actually do not and to uncritically attribute or ascribe understanding to young children, to other animals, and even to brains and computers. Furthermore, it leads educators to assess understanding through tests and texts, without considering the relation between what readers accept as making sense and what teachers insist meets the objective standards of the school. Psychologists assume that understanding is a trainable mental skill and see no need to ask what we mean by understanding. Admittedly, both scientific and educational approaches to understanding have been sufficiently successful that few have seen any necessity for asking the question. I hope to show that it is worth asking what understanding means.

"Understanding" is a verbal concept in ordinary language with a sufficiently precise meaning that it has a place in ordinary discourse. Understanding is one of a set of mentalistic concepts, including "believe," "remember," "think," and "know," that make up a "theory of mind." Nevertheless, understanding is also taken as referring to a set of cognitive processes or skills that psychologists explore by experimental means. To date, there is no exploration of the relation between these two enterprises.

I was drawn to the problem by considering understanding as an emotion, the feelings of understanding and puzzlement that we share with even infants and perhaps other animals. "Making sense," as I shall define it, is the subjective feeling of understanding, the emotional significance, value, and certainty that permits one "to go on" and that, when lacking, brings action to a halt. This subjective side of understanding is inescapable, but is the feeling of understanding what we mean by understanding?

"Understanding" – that complex faculty that puzzles philosophers and psychologists, I eventually come to argue – is little more than the knowledge of the identity conditions to be met in correctly ascribing understanding to oneself and others. This bold and somewhat opaque claim is developed in six steps throughout the book. The first two steps are fundamental, the other four spell out implications of the first two.

The first step in the analysis of understanding, I conclude, is to determine what the word "understanding" means. To learn what "understanding" means is to learn the identity conditions for the correct application of the word. I argue that the two primary identity conditions for understanding are correctness and intersubjectivity; correctness is determined by evidence, intersubjectivity by agreement between self and others. The identity conditions for the word "understand" are precisely those for the concept of understanding, thereby reducing the concept to a word meaning. The objects of understanding are expressions in a language that we may believe, as well as those that require us to withhold belief while we consider alternatives.

The second step is to ask who is doing the ascribing. This allows me to distinguish between entities that we, as adults, may ascribe understanding to, from those entities, like ourselves, capable of actually doing the ascribing. Clearly, only one in possession of the word "understand" can make ascriptions. Consequently, it may be appropriate for us as adult speakers to ascribe understanding to young children, dogs, and computers so long as their behavior meets the two criteria for understanding mentioned earlier. What those subjects cannot yet do is ascribe understanding, that is, claim, avow, or attribute understanding to themselves or others. For that, they require knowledge of how to use the word "understand." Children learn this at about six years of age and they continue to broaden their appreciation of the evidence relevant to correctness and of the expectancies of possible listeners and readers through the school years. Thus, they learn to ascribe understanding to themselves and others.

The third step is to determine why the ability to ascribe "understanding" is cognitively significant. I argue that ascription is not a mere label but a speech act, a claim about understanding that is true or false and justifiable by appeal to evidence and reason, specifically, knowing that the conditions for applying the concept of understanding have been met. Such ascriptions are, therefore, rational judgments for which the speaker is responsible.

The fourth step is to show that treating ascription of understanding as a rational judgment would explain not only the assumptions that govern everyday oral and written discourse but also those involved in the literary practices of written composition and "comprehension monitoring." Both involve self-conscious decisions as to whether or not the ascription of understanding meets the demands of correctness, as well as agreement with a possibly skeptical audience.

The fifth step is to provide some account of the cognitions and actions of creatures that we sometimes ascribe understanding to but who, as yet, are incapable of ascribing understanding. What I take away from such creatures by denying that they have concepts, I give back by acknowledging and exploring the nature of complex emotions, including the feeling of understanding. To do so, we require a concept of emotion that goes well beyond the traditional notion of emotion as pleasures and pains and grant them the cognitive richness that modern theories of emotion claim. Schacter and Singer (1962) and Oatley (1992; see also Oatley and Johnson-Laird, 1996) pointed out that feeling states are not mere tingles and buzzes but complex cognitive-emotional states with a "content" that accumulates with experience and that provides the basis for expectation as to what is likely to happen next and what to do about it. These rich cognitive-emotional states are the basic sources of behavior and they are shared with all sentient creatures. The relation between the emotional feeling of understanding and the concept of understanding is the central theme of the book.

Finally, the success of artificial intelligence (AI) in understanding language poses a new challenge to a theory of understanding. Computers that pass the Turing test are said to understand. Computer cognition serves as a stalking horse throughout this volume in that the triumphs of AI continue to astonish us and claims about computer understanding are well known, if controversial. Nonetheless, I argue that the difference between humans and computers may be explained by my distinction between "ascribed to" as opposed to "ascribed by" – that is, computers are childlike in that while it is not incorrect to ascribe understanding to them, yet as they lack a public language, they cannot ascribe understanding to themselves or others and in this way are importantly different from human understanders.

It must be pointed out that these principles were formulated not at the outset of my inquiry into understanding but rather as the outcome of the evidence and argument I consider throughout the book. For me as a writer, they are conclusions; for you as a reader, they are to serve rather as a guide through the arguments and evidence presented throughout this volume.

Understanding is one of the mental states that Descartes claimed he could not doubt. I chose that concept for two further reasons. One was that I had a long, productive, and collaborative research program at the Ontario Institute for Studies in Education of the University of Toronto (OISE/UT) on children's mental states, such as thinking, knowing, pretending, and believing, the domain now referred to the children's theory of mind, and I thought that understanding deserved a place in such an account. The second, more immediate reason was a series of interesting discussions with my friends and colleagues Keith Oatley and Brian Stock as to whether or not computers understood the languages they translated. I suspected not, not only because I agreed with John Searle's suspicions about the validity of the Turing test but also because, to me, there seemed to be an inescapable subjective feeling to understanding, a kind of consciousness of and responsibility for understanding, that computers lacked. Once I began to say why understanding had this conscious, experiential feeling – the feeling that something "makes sense" – I discovered that there is no satisfactory or agreed-upon conception of what it means to understand. Consequently, there are no clear rules for ascribing understanding either to young children or to computers. While some, primarily educators, take subjective "sense-making" as understanding, others, primarily researchers, accept only meeting an objective standard as understanding.

The conclusion I reached, as mentioned earlier, is that understanding is little more than the linguistic concept of "understanding" with rules for correct use and ascribable equally to self and others. The feeling that something makes sense provides only the motivation and confidence to persevere and the satisfactions of achievement. Thus, both conceptual knowledge and emotional commitments are important to the growth of understanding in children and to the achievement of understanding in adults.

The relationship between nonlinguistic feeling of understanding and linguistic concept of understanding may be characterized by the distinction suggested by philosopher Robert Brandom (1994) between sentience and sapience. Nonlinguistic creatures are no doubt sentient; they respond to what is going on and adapt their behavior to fulfill their desires. Only linguistic creatures are sapient in that their actions are shaped by concepts and justified by reason. Consequently, my account of cognitive development is essentially one of semantic development, learning how to use words. But what is usually seen as seamless, I see as marking a watershed. Astington and Baird (2005) asked, "How does language matter to a theory of mind?" My answer: Language permits ascription of mental states to oneself and others.

Somewhat to my surprise, I found that attribution of mental states to children was itself not innocent. The very act of attribution or, as I came to say, following the lead of my philosophical colleague, Jennifer Nagel, the act of ascription is itself important. To ascribe a trait or a property requires that one know that the criteria for correct ascription have been met. Consequently, the fundamental achievement I have been attempting to explain can be reduced to whether a state is merely ascribed to one, as in the case of young children, brains, or computers, or whether one has the ability to make the ascription, a capability I traced to knowledge of the identity conditions for the concept. Understanding is essentially knowing how to use the word "understand." I must say, I had no idea that this would be the outcome of my belabored inquiry, nor that the yield would be so modest.

Although the outcome is modest, getting there called for revolutionary changes in our (my) ideas about the mind, including a revised theory of concepts as word meanings, a new emphasis on the role of emotion in cognition, and a partial rejection of the major paradigm of the cognitive sciences, namely Representational Theory of Mind (RTM) long used to explain the cognitions of both humans and other animals.

The title of this book, *Making Sense: What It Means to Understand*, is borrowed indirectly from Marianne Janack's (2012) book *What We Mean By Experience*. The title foreshadows the conclusion I have finally reached, namely that the question as to what understanding is can be rephrased without loss as the question of what we mean by the word "understand." When I chose the title, I had no idea that my analysis would lead me there.

I hope to make clear that understanding poses not only philosophical, psychological, and developmental questions but also, equally importantly, educational ones. Understanding is both a presupposition of learning and a goal of schooling. Learners presumably rely on a feeling of understanding, that is, the feeling that what they read and hear makes sense. Yet, by emphasizing the importance of "making sense," educators may overlook the fact that understanding must also meet a standard of correctness set by the concept of understanding and monitored by the school and the larger society. Many educational debates center on a confusion as to what is meant by understanding. Educators can contribute by teaching students the differences among mental concepts such as "understanding," "knowing," and "remembering" and showing them how to judge when the ascription of understanding is warranted. This requires more than a nodding acquaintance with the word "understand" and also requires knowledge of the beliefs and expectancies of the understander and a detailed knowledge of the linguistic properties of widely diverse texts, any of which may provide evidence and reasons for the correctness of one's ascription.

The reader will recognize that my account of understanding is more a record of an inquiry, an attempt to understand a problem, than a systematic review of the relevant psychological, philosophical, or educational literatures. I review these specialist literatures primarily after I have worked out my own view. The first nine chapters in this book develop my account of understanding; the next four chapters relate my account to other accounts available in the existing literature on language, mind, and education. The final chapter, Chapter 14, reviews the uses and limitations of ascriptivism as an account of understanding and of human cognition in general.

2 Understanding As Feeling and As a Concept

Understanding takes on new meaning in the light of recent advances in children's "theory of mind" and recent advances in computer understanding of language.

INTRODUCTION

Among the few things that Descartes (2004) was certain of was that he understands: "I am a thing that thinks: that is, a thing that doubts, affirms, denies, and understands." These are the things he is, and we too are, conscious of. They make up what we think of as our minds. Yet understanding seems to be the most fundamental member of Descartes's list. Descartes's mind–body distinction and treating mind as something spiritual continues to haunt modern theories of the mind.

Locke (1829), in his famous treatise, claimed that "understanding itself is the object to be investigated," specifically "the certainty, evidence and extent of human knowledge." He continued, "Understanding is the most elevated faculty of the soul, it searches after truth and is a sense of delight [setting] man above all sensible beings." But just what is "understanding"? The editor of the 1924 edition of Locke's *Essay* inserted the footnote on the first page: "[U]nderstanding, for Locke, includes all aspects of intelligence." McDougall (1911, p. 301) argued that Locke misdiagnosed understanding because he lacked the concept of meaning. Bennett (1971), too, attributed Locke's error to his over-simple account of language. Even now, with new analysis of language and children's acquisition of language, the question of what understanding is remains uncertain. We have almost a century's worth of research on learning, memory, and comprehension, but of the experience of understanding and what we mean by understanding, little or nothing.

THE FEELING OF UNDERSTANDING

Nonetheless, I will begin, as Descartes and Locke did, and as most theorists do, by reflecting on my own subjective experience of understanding. Suppose I am looking at Magritte's famous painting of a pipe that bears the inscription "This is not a pipe." I sense a contradiction; I feel that I don't understand. When, finally, I grant that "this" refers not to the pipe but only to the picture of a pipe, I feel that I now understand that Magritte's caption is not a mistake or a lie but a kind of joke,[1] my understanding accompanied by an audible gasp, an A ha. This feeling of understanding offers one notion of what we mean by understanding. Understanding is a feeling, an emotion, evoked when the meaning of the statement is resolved to meet some standard.

My friend, standing nearby, on hearing my explanation, acknowledges that I have understood and he "ascribes" understanding to me. This ascription, by another person, offers a second notion of understanding. Understanding is a state that may be ascribed, by an observer, to someone under some conditions, primarily the condition that that person correctly understood. Evidence for correctness comes from the explanation given.

The point to be taken from this little parable is that my first-person understanding is a feeling, an emotion, whereas the ascription of understanding to me by my friend is a truth claim based on objective evidence. The theoretical question I address in what follows is

---

[1] Of course, it is more than that. Ray Jackendoff (2012), who first drew my attention to the intellectual significance of Magritte's work, pointed out that Magritte entitled this work *La trahison des images* (*The Treachery of Images*), thereby raising a fundamental question in philosophy, namely the relationship between a thing and a representation of the thing, whether as word, image, or thought, the fundamental problem of mimesis.

the relationship between first-person subjective experience of understanding and second- or third-person objective ascription of understanding. Philosophers will recognize this as the problem of "other minds." Psychologists will recognize this as a matter of comprehension and concept development. Linguists will see this as the problem of semantics, word meaning. As long as each discipline respects its own boundaries, progress is limited but assured. On the other hand, what we mean by understanding may advance by exploring the relationship amongst these different perspectives.

The feeling of understanding is the feeling that occurs when an expression, as we say, "makes sense." Although understanding language is my primary concern, such feelings appear to extend far beyond the domain of language. Feelings are manifest in the reactions of young children and other animals and provide the primary means for studying cognitive, emotional, and social behavior of creatures with or without language. To illustrate, psychologists attribute or ascribe mental states and processes to nonverbal children and other animals on the basis of where they look for displaced objects, what they orient to as novel, what they habituate to as familiar, what they respond to as equivalent, what they distinguish, and what they prefer. The study of these cognitive competencies, often described in terms of concepts and conceptual development, make up a fundamental part of developmental and animal psychology. In what follows, I describe such processes and states, not as concepts but as first-person subjective states or *feelings*, states attuned to situations that subjects are conscious of and responsive to. I describe these feeling states as emotional states in some detail in Chapter 3. Here, I simply acknowledge my assumption that understanding is an emotion that is provoked in response to language that allows one to go on.

Emotion and emotional development is an advanced field of study although it is unusual to argue that understanding may be usefully thought of as an emotion. Contrary to the more traditional assumption that the emotions are irrational forces, contemporary writers such as Lazarus (1999), Oatley (1992), and Scherer and Moors (2019) argued that emotions are complex mental processes that include sensitivity to an event or situation and an appraisal of that event in terms of prior experience and goals of the organism. In addition, an emotion involves the activation of physiological adjustments and action potentials, as well as a distinctive feeling tone. A critical part of the subjective emotional state is the appraisal of the situation in the light of prior experience, for it is that appraisal that determines the feeling evoked. Thus, the emotional state or feeling state includes what the feeling is in response to and what is to be done about it. Examples would be a fear of snakes or a desire for a drink or puzzlement at disappearing objects. Such subjective experiences, I suggest, are not thoughts; rather, they are feelings.

Language-using adults may describe their emotional states by appeal to such verbal concepts as fear, hope, interest, knowing, or understanding. Many of these states are attributed or ascribed to young children and non-speaking animals. Clearly, there is some relationship between feeling an emotion and referring to those emotions verbally. But what is that relation? There is a "Leibnizian Gap" between subjective experience and verbal concepts. On one side, we have the cognitive–emotive states I refer to as subjective feelings and, on the other, the concepts expressed by the words and sentences of a language. The two sides even have their preferred methodologies: cognitive psychology for the former, psycholinguistics for the latter. How cognitive–emotive development relates to semantic – that is, linguistic – development is, therefore, at the center of my inquiry. Specifically, what is the relationship between the feeling of understanding and the concept expressed by the word "understand," the first presumably the heritage of all animals and the second the special domain of speaking creatures?

Even if we grant the existence of a feeling of understanding, it is not clear that such a feeling is an essential part of understanding. One may feel that one understands, when, in fact, one misunderstands or does not understand. What needs to be added is some notion of correctness or truth of understanding. Understanding, like knowing, carries a notion of truth (Kiparsky & Kiparsky, 1970; Sliwa, 2015) as part of its meaning. One cannot know something false. Secondly, even if such a feeling exists, how does it inform the concept of understanding? Could one form a concept of understanding having never experienced the feeling of understanding? Conversely, does the feeling of understanding provide the meaning for the term "understand"?

Feelings are subjective, private, and experiential. For much of the past century, psychological studies of understanding have followed Locke in setting aside subjective experiences while substituting learning, remembering and thinking, and comprehending language as processes that could be objectively described and assessed. "Understanding" became "comprehension," a subtle change in meaning that, I suggest, sets aside the feeling of understanding. Comprehension, in the hands of cognitive science, came to be seen as the achievement of an objectively correct or true response. Feelings were ignored rather than actually denied. Overt, observable behavior provided an objective standard for comprehension that made an appeal to subjective feelings unnecessary. Correct answers, not sweaty palms, mattered. As subjectivity gave pride of place to objectivity, the question of how subjective feelings are related to objective knowledge lost its urgency and along with it the question of how language was related to preverbal or nonverbal cognition.

THE LANGUAGES OF THE MIND

Although Locke, Leibniz, and Hume all wrote books about understanding, it was Brentano (1973) writing in the nineteenth century who noted that concepts such as thinking, knowing, believing, and understanding are "intentional" concepts that have a unique "mark of the mental" and that deserved attention in their own right. Two lines of philosophical inquiry grew from Brentano's mentalism: one concerned with subjective feelings, the other with objective knowings. MacDonald (2012) usefully contrasted these two quite different vocabularies that have been invented for analyzing mental states.

One of these vocabularies is that of the Anglo-American "analytical" philosophers, who adopted a third-person perspective to examine the conditions under which intentional states can be correctly and objectively ascribed to any system. To ascribe a state such as believing or understanding to a system or person is to (1) attribute that state and (2) demonstrate that the state meets an objective "normative" standard of correctness for that state. That standard is set by the correct use of the term. Because ascription is in the hands of the ascriber, ascription is from a third-person point of view and it is objective in that it is assumed to meet a universalizable standard of correctness. Correctness or truth is the "normative" standard for ascribing that state. That is to say, one can ascribe understanding to a person only if they understand correctly.

The second vocabulary is that of the Phenomenological philosophers who analyze mental states from the subjective, first-person perspective of those who experience them. While the former talk of the criteria for ascribing mental states to any system, the latter talk about the conscious properties of direct experience for oneself. Analytical philosophers object to the use of introspection as a guide to knowledge. There is no love lost between these two traditions. Psychologists and educators, for their part, treat the two orientations separately. On one hand, some treat understanding as assessable objective knowledge as measured by comprehension tests. Others, especially educators (see Chapter 11), treat understanding as subjectively experienced sense-making.

Philosophers working in the analytical tradition disparage, or dismiss completely, the importance of the first, the subjective perspective. Hume (1993), suspicious of "visions" and religious inspirations, vigorously dismissed introspection as a reliable method for investigating mental states. Popper (1972) dismissed the relevance of such first-person feelings by arguing that psychological states are too private and subjective to serve as a basis for objective knowledge. He would, presumably, also dismiss as unreliable my self-report of the feelings I experienced when viewing Magritte's pipe picture.

Wittgenstein (1953), who is credited with shifting the study of the mind to the study of the language of the mind, suggested that we ask not what subjective mental states are but how we ascribe mental terms to people. He wrote:

> Try not to think of understanding as a "mental process" at all. For *that* is the expression which confuses you. But ask yourself: in what sort of case, in what kind of circumstances, do we say, "Now I know how to go on." (p. 154)

Psychologists (me) tend to simply dismiss Wittgenstein's advice and explain cognitive states such as believing and understanding in terms of mental representation and operations on those representations appealing to some form of the Representational Theory of Mind (RTM). Analytical philosophers, on the other hand, largely follow Wittgenstein's notion of ascription of mental states and what they call the "identity criteria" or conditions to be met in ascribing them. As these criteria are objective, there is little place for the first-person subjective feelings, including the feeling of understanding. Although Davidson (2001), whose views I consider in more detail in Chapter 14, acknowledged the directness of first-person subjective states, he denied the relevance of those feeling states to the ascription of mental states, since the ascription to either self or other must, he claimed, meet the same objective identity criteria. This denial of subjectivity is unacceptable to developmental psychologists and all child watchers; children are nothing if not in thrall to their subjectivity, a subjectivity that observers believe they share with their subjects. Infants, like all animals, feel hunger and sense danger even if they, lacking language, cannot ascribe hunger or fear to anyone. One of the problems for developmental psychology, as I see it, is to sort out the relationship between such feelings and the concepts they acquire for representing them.

Ascribing a mental state such as believing or understanding on the basis of objective criteria without regard for subjective feelings has an important advantage. It would allow one to ascribe such states to any system that meets the objective criteria for that state. For believing and understanding the primary normative condition is truth or correctness, getting it right. That is, an observer or tester could claim that a person understands if that person provides relevant evidence for understanding such as passing a test. The same objective criteria used in ascribing understanding to adult humans could then be used to ascribe understanding to brain states, computers, animals, and young children so long as they performed in a certain way. This, of course, is the guiding principle for both designing objective tests to measure understanding and for attributing intelligence to machines (AI).

However, this may trigger an "ascription fallacy," in analogy to "attribution fallacy" of psychological traits, where it has been found that others are willing to attribute states and traits to clients that the clients themselves, if asked, may reject. That is, an ascription fallacy would occur if the criteria for recognizing and ascribing the state are inadequate or inappropriate. It could be argued, as I later shall, that an important aspect of understanding is a system's ability to ascribe that state to itself or others. Similarly, it could be argued, though I shall later question it, that understanding be ascribed only if that state evokes an appropriate feeling of understanding. Finally, it could be argued that understanding may be correctly ascribed only if understanding is distinguished, not only from misunderstanding but also from related mental states such as believing, remembering, and knowing. If young children fail to make such distinctions, perhaps we should not ascribe such states to them. Hence, much depends on how one sets the criteria to be met in ascribing a mental state. To date, ascriptivists prefer objective, behavioral criteria to subjective ones, subjectivists the reverse.

REDEFINING THE PROBLEM
Conjecture 1. Rather than treating subjective feelings and objective criteria as competing theories, we may begin by considering them as alternative grounds for attributing or ascribing understanding. That is,

subjective feelings may provide one basis for the ascription of under-standing to oneself as an "avowal." Meeting the objective or "norma-tive" standard of correctness is the other. Setting aside for the moment, the important difference between feeling a state and avowing it, it could be suggested that one could avow understanding – "I get it" – on the basis of a certain feeling or emotional state, or one could demonstrate understanding by correctly answering questions, judging truth, or providing an explanation. Whereas the feeling of understanding is personal and subjective, that of answering questions is objective and public. Subjective feelings and objective performances may point, in their different ways, to a common mental event: under-standing. The question would thereby shift from feelings and ascrip-tions to the question of what understanding is as a mental state or process. In this way, one could hand the problem of understanding back to the psychologists and out of the hands of the philosophers.

As appealing as this view is, I now see it as having critical faults. First, an avowal is a verbal act that reaches out beyond the experience itself into the world of language. Nonlinguistic children and other creatures cannot avow. Introspection is already a linguistic act that may refer to a certain state but is not to be identified with that state. Thus, there may not be any one mental state of under-standing pointed to by both subjective experience and objective evidence. There is a second problem. Emotional states are causal states lacking "normativity," whereas the concept of understanding assumes the normative status of truth or correctness. So I suggest that the feeling of understanding cannot serve as the meaning of the concept of understanding.

Conjecture 2. There is no unique feeling or process that defines understanding. Rather, understanding is knowledge of a linguistic concept defined in terms of the identity conditions for the correct ascription of understanding. Learning these conditions makes up a major part of conceptual development. This is a fraught conclusion, and I explore and defend it in greater detail in Chapters 3, 4, and 5.

COGNITIVE PROCESSES INVOLVED IN LEARNING
TO ASCRIBE UNDERSTANDING

Cognitive psychologists, among whom I number myself, unlike phil-osophers, are suspicious of "conceptual analysis," the attempt to define mental terms by analysis and reflection. Rather than reflect on what the words "thinking" and "understanding" mean, we set out to examine what thinkers are doing (Bruner, Goodnow & Austin, 1956). This was one of the roots of cognitive science, a discipline that attempts to bridge cognition, language, and computationalism (Pylyshyn, 1984). Unlike Behaviorism that denied mental processes altogether, the cognitive sciences attempt to explain beliefs and meanings, in some cases by reducing them to computational brain processes, algorithms[2] that operate largely outside of consciousness (Engleman, 2011). In other cases, the one chosen here, one frames explanations in ordinary language terms such as meanings, beliefs, and intentions. While mental processes are brain processes, and brain processes may be described or modeled as computable associative and algorithmic processes, these analyses fail to capture the subjective feelings that humans experience. Computationalists, like the Behaviorists before them, do not consider this as a loss.

UNDERSTANDING LANGUAGE

"Understanding" applies equally to understanding the world, under-standing object permanence, for example, as well as to understanding the meaning of an utterance or a text. Locke and his heirs never pursued this distinction (Bennett, 1971). While claiming to examine human understanding, Locke focused attention on the nature and sources of knowledge rather than on the relationship between

---

[2] Algorithms are procedures that are mechanically applied, that is, that do not originate with conscious thought. I use the term to apply both to rules as in traditional AI and to the pattern recognition associative networks employed in ML systems, while acknowledging the important differences between them. Cognitivists (me) see algorithms as learned rules that may be applied in solving problems and offer long division as emblematic.

knowledge and the language in which knowledge is represented. In the early nineteenth century, a clear distinction emerged between explanation (understanding nature) and understanding (grasping meanings of language) and so making a clear distinction, as they put it, between reading the book of scripture and reading the book of nature (Olson, 1994). The former – reading, a linguistic activity – is my primary concern here: "understanding" is correctly grasping the meaning of an expression. Only with language, I suggest, does the problem of meaning arise and with it a possible distinction between meaning and belief. One can understand expressions that one does not believe.

For Locke, knowing was synonymous with understanding. Words simply pointed to ideas understood as faint copies of objects in the world. The meaning of words and sentences came in for modern disciplined study in the nineteenth century in the hands of humanist philosophers who, following the leads of Kant and Hegel, created the field of hermeneutics. Concerned with bringing some rigor into biblical interpretation, they attempted to show how valid interpretation could be "grounded openly" in the text (Gadamer, 1975). Thus, they distinguished the structural properties of the text, "the wordless and authorless object," from "the enactment of the semantic possibilities of the text" (Ricoeur, 1981, p. 152,159), the possible relations to a reader's beliefs, thereby both conferring a degree of autonomy to the linguistic expression and a new awareness of the problems of interpretation. In my own words, these scholars showed how textual and contextual evidence could be used to justify or validate interpretation and root out inspiration and epiphany as modes of knowledge. For the hermeneuticists, the existence and autonomy of linguistic structure was premised on the objective physical presence of a written form that can be visually inspected and reread. Hence, it is no surprise that hermeneutics was created for dealing with written texts even if the model developed could also be applied to spoken language.[3]

---

[3] The role of writing in creating a modern "textual" culture has been discussed by Stock (1983) and Olson (1994).

Correct interpretation of texts also came to be seen as the central concern of education. Johann Herbart (1893), a Kantian educational theorist writing in the early nineteenth century, advanced a theory of understanding text as "apperception," a kind of second-order perception. He attempted to explain not what learners encountered in a stimulus or text but rather what they "took up" from their experience. Apperception involves fitting textual information into an already established cognitive system. Apperception was not to be confused with ordinary perception or those forms of learning that humans share with other animals. Rather, apperception pertains primarily to human learning through language, to reseeing the world in terms of linguistic categories.

Contemporary psychological studies of understanding written texts adopt the Herbart–hermeneutics distinction between the text and its appropriation but set aside the humanist concern with the reader's subjective experience of understanding. The shift, I suggested, is marked by renaming the field of study "comprehension." Miller (1979) pointed out that in reading a text, as in hearing an utterance, one carries out two concurrent but separable processes. One builds a model, a textual image, of the text at some level of generality, whether merely as visual image or as a grammatical string of words and letters. The second process, like Herbart's apperception, is the uptake of the text, the further step of relating the textual image to one's prior knowledge, context, and goals to form a model of the text, that is, of what the text "means."

The comprehension processes involved in reading words, sentences, and simple texts has been the subject of a generation of extensive empirical studies. Kintsch (1998) summarized these studies, integrating them in terms of what he called a Construction–Integration model, a computational model consisting of a set of algorithmic procedures applied to the structure of the text to form a structured textbase, essentially parsing the sentence, which, in turn, is related to the concurrent knowledge and goals of the reader, to form what he calls a situation model.[4] That situation model is the outcome of the comprehension process. More controversial is the claim that if his simulation meets the same objective criteria, correctness, that human subjects do, it may be said to understand. Understanding is ascribed to both the simulation and to humans even if for humans, understanding is accompanied by a feeling of understanding, namely the feeling that a text makes sense to a reader who takes to be true or possibly true. For a human to understand is to form a belief as to what a text means.

The distinction between the textual image and the apprehended image is widely acknowledged in the literature and is important to what follows. Distinctions between "sentence meaning" versus "speaker's meaning" (Grice, 1989), sense versus reference (Frege in Dummett, 1993), "semantic structure" versus meaning (Jackendoff, 2002, 2012), and "what is said" and "what is meant" (Olson, 1977) all capture this distinction. Theories of comprehension, such as those of Miller and Kintsch, offer a general account of how readers manage these constraints in understanding a text although none of them ask the question as to what we mean by understanding, that is, how understanding is ascribed to anyone. Moreover, all such theories plant the assumption that creating the image of the text precedes, and is independent of, the assignment of meaning, an assumption I reject in Chapter 5.

THREE CHALLENGES TO COGNITIVE THEORIES OF UNDERSTANDING

Three developments in the cognitive sciences offer new perspectives on understanding. One was the discovery in the 1980s that children acquired a consciousness of mind as manifest by the ability to attribute false beliefs to others only when they were four or five years of age. This achievement is usually traced to the acquisition of a concept

---

[4] Kintsch acknowledged that no algorithm exists for parsing a text. As I understand it, only humans can translate a situation and a sentence into a common format such that the two may be compared.

of belief, one of the concepts that make up a "theory of mind," concepts including think, know, wonder, believe, imagine, pretend, and understand. An important feature of such concepts, including understanding, is that they are attributable or "ascribable" equally to self and other. The second is a recent advance in AI in the form of machine learning (ML), systems that can learn and process language to a level of sophistication that appears to warrant the ascription of understanding to the computer. The third is the challenge to the very notion of mental representation posed by Wittgenstein's suggestion, as developed in the writings of Donald Davidson (2001) and others, that we focus rather on the linguistic practices involved in ascribing mental states. This third unfolds throughout the volume. For now, I focus on the first two, the mental states of young children and computers. Consider them in turn.

CHILDREN'S THEORY OF MIND

As children approach school age, the age at which they almost universally are said to "get sense," they acquire a competence with some of the very notions that Descartes took as manifesting mind. They come to recognize that they and others think, doubt, wonder, imagine, and understand. With this understanding of mind comes the ability to recognize that others may believe something that they themselves know to be false but also to tell lies, make promises, recognize misunderstandings, keep secrets, play make-believe games, and experience a variety of complex cognitive emotions such as shame and embarrassment, pride, and disappointment. These achievements appear to be associated with the acquisition of language, although the specific role that language plays remains a focus of ongoing research (Astington & Baird, 2005; see also Astington, Harris & Olson, 1988; Wellman, Cross & Watson, 2001). I review some of the research evidence on this point in Chapter 10.

Children's understanding of mind is closely tied, in a way yet to be examined, to the acquisition of concepts of mind that may be expressed in a language for talking about what was said and meant, thought, and believed. That is, those who understand that they them-selves or someone else may entertain a false belief also tend to know and correctly use the word "think" (Montgomery, 2005; Lockl & Schneider, 2016). The genius of the original Wimmer and Perner's (1983) "false belief" study was that it avoided using the word "think" in the task, asking rather "where Maxi would look" for a displaced object, thereby defining the task as a cognitive rather than a linguistic achievement. Yet it may be argued that employing the word "think" appropriately is precisely what is required for ascribing a mental state to Maxi. The subjectively held cognitive state or concept that allows the child to predict the actions of another is, in a way I shall attempt to make clear, identical to the semantic knowledge that permits the correct use of a word for ascribing a belief. If true, this suggests that one may examine children's mental states by examining the seman-tics of mental terms. This is the route I propose to follow in my account of understanding, namely to determine the conditions under which the lexical concept of understanding may be correctly applied by and to children. In so doing, the question shifts from understanding as a cognitive process to the linguistic problem of how to use the word "understand" (Olson & Astington, 1986). In this I take heed of Wittgenstein's injunction to attend, not to mental processes but to how mental terms are used. At the same time, I acknowledge that talk of word meanings seems to hide or ignore the rich knowledge that children bring to the language-learning episode (Nelson, 2005). As one critic noted, concepts do not just spring up in response to a phono-logical cue; the learner brings to mind something to distinguish one concept from another and something for the new concept to refer to and that is usefully designated by the term.

Second, children's understanding of false belief, or, as I would now prefer to say, their ability to ascribe belief, provides a model for ascribing understanding. That is, evidence on which one bases the ascription of belief to a child is the child's ability to ascribe false belief. So, too, for understanding; the best evidence that children have a concept of understanding is their competence in recognizing and ascribing misunderstanding. I examine this point in detail in Chapter 8.

An immediate objection to seeing mental concepts as word meanings that permit ascription is that long before children acquire a language of mind, they manifest a range of complex cognitive–emotional feeling states, including feelings of glee at mildly surprising events such as "peek-a-boo," mild distress at unfocused images, boredom with repetition, puzzlement at anomalies, all of which may be taken as indications of understanding and its contrary. More importantly, they follow orders, answer questions, or enjoy listening to stories, all of which imply some beliefs and some understanding of language. It seems axiomatic that understanding precedes the linguist concept of understanding. To explain this apparent contradiction, it will be necessary to set out a clearer notion of what we mean by understanding and then see how the concept is applied to young children and, more importantly, how the concept is acquired and used by the children themselves. Only then can I set out how the feeling of understanding relates to acquisition of the concept of understanding. I explore this relation more fully in Chapter 7.

MACHINE LEARNING AND UNDERSTANDING

The second, new perspective on language and language understanding that prompts this enquiry comes from a new form of AI called ML (Machine Learning) that has been developed by Hinton (2007, 2014) and others. Unlike traditional AI, in which the computer is programmed to achieve particular ends, ML essentially trains itself. Provided with simple algorithms, extensive computational resources, and massive data sets, ML computers are able to organize data into associative patterns that allow for prediction. Thus, each bit of input is anticipated by, rather than merely responded to, by the program (Clark, 2013; Kuperberg & Jaeger, 2016). The achievements of ML are impressive indeed and include the ability, not only to answer questions but also to learn language to a level capable of translating from one natural language into another, an achievement that would seem to justify the ascription of understanding language to a computer (Jackendoff, 2012, p. 46).[5]

I take ML to have demonstrated two properties of language learning that had previously remained speculative. First, ML extends traditional AI in demonstrating that computational procedures, this time in the form of associative networks, may explain important aspects of language learning, namely learning the "semantic structure," the network of relations within the linguistic system. The semantic structure is internal to the language and independent of reference. Recall that ML systems are exposed only to strings of linguistic expressions rather than to perceptual interactions with the world. Thus, I take ML programs to have demonstrated the possibility of learning the *sense* of the language, that is, the meanings *in* the language, independently of reference, that is, the way that the world is taken to be.

Second, ML demonstrates how any cognitive state is a joint product of the input and prior state of the system. More precisely, the prior state of the system provides the given in terms of which any new input is perceived. By the "given," I mean not the stimulus but what a subject holds to be true or real and expected. Much of cognitive psychology of the past half century, indexed by Bruner's "new look" in perception (Anglin, 1973), was devoted to showing how prior knowledge in the form of "top-down" processes such as expectancies, plans, schema, scripts, or mental models, interacted with "bottom-up" processes, those activated by the senses, to form a response. While confirming what cognitive psychologists had long claimed, ML demonstrated that such effects are pervasive and could be achieved mechanically, that is, computationally.

One astonishing confirmation of the power of the background of expectancies on perception comes from a brain study that found that

---

[5] Bronte used the same criterion: "I was making her translate currently from English to French ... by way of ascertaining that she comprehended what she had read" (C. Bronte, *Villette*, p. 67).

neurons in the fusiform face recognition area (FFA) respond every bit as strongly to non-face stimuli (in this experiment, house) under high expectation of faces, as they do to face stimuli. That is, under special conditions, the part of the brain specialized for face recognition is activated by a non-face stimulus, a house (Egner, Monti & Summerfield, 2010)! Thus, the brain is doing just what Peter Wason's (1980) human subjects were doing when they described a red square as "not blue," which they did when a red one follows a string of blues. In more general terms, a stimulus is never just a stimulus; a stimulus is experienced in terms of the preexisting state of the system.

Drawing inferences about human cognition from AI is, at best, controversial. There appears to be little agreement amongst AI researchers themselves as to what computers are actually doing. Computer Scientist Carl Miller (2018) and others (AIweirdness.com) claim that ML systems process linguistic expressions without understanding the meanings of the words they process. Further, some claim that it is difficult or impossible to know how translations were generated. Miller writes, "Algorithms are able to handle an unfathomably complex world better than a human can ... But, the way they work has become unfathomable too ... it is possible that no one knows exactly what they're doing" (New Yorker interview, October 14, 2019).

ML technology now includes not only reading and translating but also writing. Ilya Sutskever, chief scientist of Open AI, the developer of the ML writing program GPT-2a that, given a suitable start, can create text, admitted thus: "We don't really know what it means for a system to understand something, and when you look at a system like this it can be genuinely hard to tell ... researchers can't disallow the possibility that we will reach understanding when the neural net gets as big as the brain." On the contrary, we may be able to tell only when we have a more adequate account of what it means to understand.

Ron Baecker (2019) points out that unlike old-fashioned AI that built systems out of logical relations between facts, recent ML systems represent knowledge in complex assemblies of low-level processing units with hundreds of thousands of units contributing to any response. "Applicable methods for knowing what such a system knows or does not know" are lacking. He adds, "[I]f we don't understand how an AI system works, we cannot trust it ... or hold it accountable." It is worth noting that we humans too often have little understanding of how our minds come up with beliefs and hunches. The inability of computers to give reasons is shared with many students who are often unable to give reasons for their answers, the bane of teachers everywhere. Yet, by responding correctly, ML systems provide objective evidence that would seem to warrant the ascription of understanding to them even if they can neither justify their responses nor actually believe them to be true.

Thus, attributing understanding to a brain or to a computer is problematic. Even if such processes are carried out computationally, humans experience such confirmations and violations of expectations in terms of feeling of surprise, alarm, satisfaction, interest, understanding, and making sense. These feelings may play a role in learning generally and they may constitute the intuitions that feed, in some way, into explicit concepts.[6] ML appears to achieve the same output as human subjects but without any such feelings. On the other hand, as we have seen, feelings are subjective, and ascribing understanding on the basis of feelings may or may not be warranted in that one may, in fact, misunderstand. ML programs have no subjective feelings but they meet objective criteria, that is, the normative standard, in this case giving answers and correctly translating between languages.

CORRECTNESS AS A NORMATIVE STANDARD
FOR UNDERSTANDING

The Turing test (Turing, 1950) is the most famous of these objective tests for inferring and attributing intelligence to computers. Turing argued that the question as to whether computers can think or not is "meaningless" and offered in its place the objective criterion of

---

[6] I am indebted to Keith Oatley for this important suggestion.

success in imitating human performance. Turing's prediction that computer's intellectual achievements could one day be indistinguishable from or surpass those of humans is no longer in question. IBM's Watson's success at the show Jeopardy! is only one among many demonstrations that computers routinely surpass humans in meeting objective standards, thus warranting, some say, the ascription of intelligence to computers.

Critics have noted that behavioral criteria, such as those of the Turing test, are a legacy of Behaviorism (Carruthers, 1996; Stanford Encyclopedia of Philosophy, 2006), the tradition that, in principle, excluded appeal to internal states such as meaning and belief. John Searle (1979, 1983) objected that language translation could be achieved without understanding if one had access to a codebook that paired equivalent expressions. Searle insisted that consciousness, lacking in computers, plays an irreducible role of, in human cognition, an insistence that has been largely ignored.

More recently, Marianne Janack (2012) provided an extensive critique of the computer as a model of the mind. She decried the "retreat from the first-person perspective and the concepts of agency, intentionality and the mental that are tied to it. This retreat, [she writes] which Rorty and Quine explicitly champion, marks the methodologies of both behaviorism and computationalism (pp. 69–70)." She rejects both while offering an account of first-person subjective experience as an alternative to explanations based on either stimulus sensations or social discourse.

My proposal borrows in large part from Janack's defense of first-person subjective experience. Janack rejects the computational model of mind because it "misses the essential role of agency and normativity in understanding how language and 'the world' come together" (pp. 78–79). With Janack, I would argue that computers lack the first-person subjective state needed to bring "language and the world together." By excluding feelings and avowals, the Turing test at best meets a behavioral symptom of understanding without linking understanding to belief. Nonetheless, computers appear to meet the objective criteria for understanding; they do give a correct answer.

However, in my view, Janack fails to distinguish subjective experience from the avowals of that experience and, consequently, leaves unresolved just how first-person subjective experience relates to a third-person objective account and consequently of how the feeling of understanding is related to the concept of understanding. A more promising account of the relationship between subjective experience and objective, conceptual knowledge comes from another analytical philosopher, Joelle Proust (2014). In her important analysis of children's mental states, she distinguishes the objective achievement of the cognitive system, what I called "correctness," from the subjective "feeling of knowing" that is involved in appraising cognitive states and processes. The feeling of knowing – that is, noetic feelings, she argues – is associated with novelty or familiarity and provides "epistemic guidance" to animals and young children as well as to higher forms of normative assessment such as an adult's awareness of the need for justification. I interpret her metacognitive system as part of what I have referred to as the subjective feeling system and her objective knowledge system as the product of learning concepts expressed in a public language. I return to her important proposal in later chapters. The strength of Proust's proposal is that it gives place both to feelings and objective correctness rather than forcing a choice between them.

The problem in ascribing intelligence to machines was created when Turing himself suggested that the question of attribution of thinking (and meaning) should be replaced by asking if the computer meets an objective criterion, namely a performance indistinguishable from that of a thinking person. The substitution of an objective criterion for a subjective one was, as noted, the breakthrough to AI. Nevertheless, by replacing the concept of "thinking" with an objective performance, Turing may have subtly changed the question. Similarly, by replacing "understanding" by predicting, Sutskever may have changed the question. Does the science of mind require an account of subjective mental states and feelings, or can mind be reduced to meeting objective criteria, namely successful outcomes? I note in passing the affinity between Turing's and Wittgenstein's substitutions of objective criteria for subjective ones.

What is overlooked, I suggest, is the intimate relationship between the experience and, later, the avowal of understanding for oneself, Janack's concern, and the ascription of understanding to others, a concern best articulated in the writings of Donald Davidson (2001, chapter 14). The feeling of understanding for oneself may be an essential condition for ascribing that state to oneself or, indeed, to others. As computer scientists such as Miller, Sutskever, or Baecker make no claim that computers either experience or avow understanding, perhaps understanding should not be ascribed to them. It depends upon what we mean by understanding. Is understanding a subjective experience or an objective outcome? Along the lines of Conjecture 2 (mentioned earlier), I propose to reconceive this problem in terms of the identity conditions for ascribing the concept of understanding (Chapter 7).

Whereas computers appear to understand language without belief, young children appear to have beliefs without concepts of belief. Yet both seem to pose problems for ascribing understanding – one by an excess of subjectivity, the other with an excess of objectivity. Both hinge on the role of language, to which I now turn.

3   The Linguistic Basis of Mind

Understanding is both a mental process and a linguistic concept. Language allows the formation of thoughts without necessarily believing them. Furthermore, the linguistic concepts of belief and understanding have normative properties, such as truth and goodness, that appear to go beyond the cognitive states of young children and other animals.

Modern linguists, like the hermeneuticists before them, insist that language is an autonomous, self-contained system, a module, in which components, whether phonological, semantic, or grammatical, are represented in terms of each other – /b/ differs from /p/ by a single feature "voiced"; bachelor differs from male adult by the feature "married," and so on (Jackendoff, 2002). As Saussure (1958) put it, "In language there are only differences." Although, in humans, learning a language appears to also depend on knowledge of the world of reference, what is learned is a language, "an autonomous system existing in the mind" (Katz & Fodor, 1963). These linguistic structures – technically "semantic structures" or Fregean *senses*, are the meanings *in* the language that exist quite independently of the ways that those semantic structures refer to the world. Thus, *senses* are not merely signs; they are meanings defined in terms of each other – dog as an animal, green as a color, up as opposed to down, and so on.

In some early research on children's language (Olson, 1970), I asked young children to tell another child which of two blocks a star was hidden under. The star was always under the same block. All that varied was the other block that accompanied the critical block. It turned out that the child's answer was determined by the accompanying block. The results are shown in Figure 3.1.

	Event	Alternative	Utterance
Case 1	○	●	... the white one
Case 2	○	■	... the round one
Case 3	○	□ ● ■	... the round, white one
Case 4	○		... (look under) the round, white, wooden block that is about one inch across...

FIGURE 3.1 The effect of context.
Source: Adapted from Olson, D. R. (1970). Language and thought: A cognitive theory of semantics. Psychological Review, 77, 257–272. Permission from APA applied for.

When in the presence of a black block, the children said, "It's under the white one; whereas in the presence of the square block, the children said, "It's under the round one." Thus, how the object was named depended on the context of alternatives. My purpose at the time was to show how the context determined how the reference object was represented in language. Unknowingly, I had rediscovered Frege's sense-reference distinction. "The white one" and "the round one" have different senses but refer to the same physical object. What I failed to recognize at the time was that what the children were learning was not something about the blocks but rather what "white" and "round" meant, words that can be carried over and applied to new reference objects. Learning language necessarily involves making a sense-reference distinction, that is, learning what words "mean," as well as what they may refer to.

What they have left to learn are the relations among these terms, namely that white contrasts with black and both are colors, that round contrasts with square and both are shapes. These relations make up the semantic field of related concepts even if young children at first recognize only few of these relations. When I asked young children "What is the opposite of white," they often claimed not to know. Yet when I told them "black," they often were immediately able to answer "small" to the question "What is the opposite of 'big'?" I infer that the words were not known as isolated entities but part of a network even if the dimension of that network had to be elaborated, often through systematic education. Similarly, young children when asked what "big" means, they may report "elephant," providing the referent rather than the meaning. Yet clearly they know the meaning as well as the referent, as they are able to apply the word to new objects of the same kind.

There is some controversy as to whether Vygotsky grasped the sense-reference distinction. Both Fodor (1972) and Wertsch (2000) have argued that he did not. Vygotsky (1986, pp. 222–224) had claimed that when children were asked about a word, they pointed to the reference object. He wrote, "[T]he word to the child is an integral part of the object" and again that "the meaning of a word is a complex of concrete objects connected by a factual tie." Vygotsky advanced the notion of "scientific concepts," those acquired in school, to explain how and when terms came to be defined in terms of each other rather than in terms of their referents. I return to this topic in Chapter 10 where I review complimentary evidence from alternative research traditions. For now it is sufficient to note that young children can apply their verbal concepts to new objects and in that way distinguish sense from reference.

The independence of meaning from reference is what structuralists from Saussure to Chomsky (1969) have insisted on, and that I have taken ML to have demonstrated. How, then, are these autonomous linguistic structures related to cognitive states such as expectations and beliefs? Learning a language is working out the relationship between the semantic structures of the language with its nouns, verbs, subjects, and predicates (Bogden, 2009) and the cognitive or affective knowledge of nonlinguistic creatures and that which pre-linguistic children bring to language learning. This is the cognition–semantics problem.

Children's learning to use language to refer to objects and events is similar in principle to learning to use language to refer to expressions in the language rather than to objects and events. Among children's early words are "ask," "say," and "tell" (Chomsky, 1969), which are soon to be broadened to include the more specific concepts such as "promise," "claim," "lie," and "think." "Understand" is a member of this class of nominal verbs for talking about one's reaction to what is said. The fact that the reference of such terms is a linguistic object rather than a physical one led some philosophers such as Descartes to see the reference of such expressions as metaphysical or spiritual entities separate from the corporal reality of bodies. Rather, the reference for thought and understanding is simply more language.

In view of the remarkable achievements of pre-linguistic children and nonlinguistic primates, it may seem that little is added by semantic development. Thus, one could claim that learners may act appropriately without concepts or that they possess concepts but lack the necessary words for expressing them or have the concept applicable to their own experience but are unable to apply the concept to others. In regard to understanding, I will argue that, in fact, there are only two basic questions: what precisely do we mean by the word "understand" and, second, what is involved in ascribing understanding. Consider them in turn.

WHAT "UNDERSTANDING" MEANS

"Understanding" is a word among a set of words, such as "meaning" and "believing," that name and express a set or network of concepts for talking about what we say, think, and do, a competence we may describe as possessing a theory of mind. Thus, a person understands an expression when the word "understand" may be applied or ascribed to that person correctly.

Second, "understand" is a word in a public, socially shared language with a distinct *sense*. What makes up the *sense* of the word "understand" remains to be determined. I nominate two features or "identity criteria" as defining the word "understand"; the first is correctness or truth, the second intersubjectivity. I defend these features later, but, in general, the first feature, truth or correctness, is required to distinguish "understanding" from "misunderstanding," as well as to distinguish expressions that make sense from those that do not. The second feature, intersubjectivity, comes from a fact that language is a shared, public system of communication. A public language is necessarily designed for shared public use; words by their very nature have a first-person, third-person equivalence. As we shall see, these two identity conditions are not interdependent in that the normative standard for truth or correctness also depends on self–other agreement as to what may serve as evidence or reason for correctness. Consequently, assessing truth and negotiating agreements may call for an extended education.

Third, the significance of a public language was made clear by Wittgenstein (1958) in his famous "private language" argument. He claimed that a private language was not possible because without confirmation by others, there is no way to know if one was following the rule or convention for applying the concept – that is, there is no way to judge correctness for use of the concept except by confirmation by others. The private language argument would rule out private mental concepts in general and the Representational Theory of Mind (RTM) in particular. In denying private concepts, I am denying the possibility of nonlinguistic concepts.

Fourth, understanding is a concept in a natural, socially shared public language that makes reference to a shared world that includes not only objects but also feelings, beliefs, and linguistic expressions. Children's cognitive development is in part learning that shared language for talking about a shared world. When children have learned to

use the word "understand," they have learned how to ascribe understanding to themselves and others and how to sort out expressions
that are understood from those that are not. Self-ascription, as
opposed to having understanding ascribed to one, I will argue, is the
decisive step in the development of and the very experience
of understanding.

Here I take encouragement from Davidson's (2001) famous
claim that there are no beliefs without a concept of belief, thereby
denying that preverbal children and simpler animals have beliefs.
I propose the parallel, austere claim that there is no state or process
of understanding, without the linguistic concept of understanding.
Yet, as we shall see in Chapters 8 and 12, we may ascribe understanding to systems that lack requisite concept; this apparent contradiction
will be resolved when I consider in more detail the difference between
the states we ascribe *to* children as opposed to the same states
ascribed *by* children.

The linguistic concept of understanding, as part of a socially
shared public language, would help to explain the symmetry between
self-ascription and the objectively correct understanding, between
ascriptions and avowals, and between concepts[1] and words.

ASCRIBING UNDERSTANDING

In regard to the second question, considerable progress has been made
by philosophers in explaining how we ascribe mental states and how
we distinguish among them. Rozeboom (1972) was among the first to
point out the distinctions between thinking and perceiving and
believing. He argued that whereas perception ordinarily involves an
updating of beliefs – "seeing is believing" – only linguistic expressions
allow one to entertain, that is, to understand, an expression without

---

[1] I continue to use the word "concept" not as a mental state independent of language
but as an acknowledgment that synonyms and work-arounds may express the same
meaning that the prototypical word does – for example, "get it" is a synonym of
"understand." I argue that concepts are word meanings.

actually believing it. Entertaining, rather than believing, a statement allows one to think rather than to act.

Bertrand Russell had earlier distinguished understanding from believing (1948, p. 115).[2] He wrote, "I incline to the view that believing a sentence is a simpler occurrence than understanding without belief; I think the primitive reaction is belief, and that understanding without belief involves inhibition of the impulse to belief." Understanding, that is, forming a new belief on the basis of an expression rather than simply assimilating an expression to what was already known, is both a later achievement and a feature that distinguishes the concept of understanding from the concept of believing. Although both Rozeboom and Russell themselves clearly possessed the concepts they ascribed, neither asked whether their imagined subjects also possessed those concepts or the ability to ascribe them to others. Their ascriptions are purely objective.

Leslie (1987) argued that young children's early ability to pretend that a banana was a telephone was an early indication of the separation of the meaning of the word "telephone" from its normal reference. Put another way, Leslie ascribed pretense to young children but it is not clear whether the children also had a concept of pretense, although some evidence supports that possibility (Malvestuto-Felice, 1986).

Johnson and Maratsos (1977) examined children's developing understanding of the mental concepts expressed by the words "think" and "know." Young children were satisfied that they "knew" if they guessed correctly. Older children made the distinction. Critics noted that the study of the meaning of words leaves open the possibility that

---

[2] It was sheer coincidence that I came across Russell's (1948) suggestion that belief preceded understanding, in a yellowing copy of his book *Human Knowledge: Its Scope and Limits* on my shelf, well after I had clumsily formulated my proposal. His commitment to ordinary language explanations in terms of understanding and belief as an alternative to my more cumbersome notions of cognitive and semantic structure helped greatly in clarifying my view. Surely, Russell had no premonition that his intuition that believing is easier than understanding without believing would, almost a century later, predict a fact about children's language development, namely that they can entertain and attribute a false belief without themselves believing it.

children possessed the concepts all along and only later learned the correct use of mental words. I reject that criticism by arguing that the word's meaning is the concept.

The relationship between the word and the concept first became clear in Wimmer and Perner's (1983) "false belief" task. They bypassed the word "think" by asking where someone holding a false belief would look for a hidden object, a task children solved in the late preschool years. Their finding encouraged the view that children possessed the concept quite independently of the word "think." The later study by Gopnik and Astington (1988) showed that these two tasks, knowing where to look and ascribing belief, were essentially equivalent. Children who could attribute false belief could also ascribe false belief; understanding false belief, the attribution of the belief, and the ascription of the belief were closely related, if not identical – that is, the ability to understand false belief depends upon knowledge of the word "think."

A similar case may be made for the concept of understanding. Robinson, Goelman and Olson (1983) provided some evidence that children learn to distinguish understanding from misunderstanding only when they learn the word "understand." Specifically, younger children claimed that they or their listener understood an utterance even if it was incomplete or ambiguous so long as it was not false. Older children recognized the possibility of misunderstanding, pointing out the ambiguity or incompleteness of the statement. Yet it remains unclear if the ability to understand, the concept of under- standing, and knowledge of the word "understand" are as interrelated as I have suggested. I consider these possibilities more fully in Chapter 8.

Understanding is both something we do and a concept in a language. Language is doubly implicated in that what we understand are linguistic expressions, and, furthermore, we again use language to talk about what we understand. Consequently, understanding is essentially talk about talk. Both rely on the conventions in the lan- guage. Yet it is both tempting and conventional to think of understanding as a general cognitive faculty. The alternative is to consider the possibility that it is language all the way down.

To foreshadow what is to come, it will be necessary to raise the further question of who is doing the ascribing. To correctly ascribe understanding obviously requires that the speaker know the word and the concept "understand." There is no necessity that the child to whom understanding is ascribed also possesses the concept. But at the same time, the target of our investigation is to examine how the child acquires the ability to ascribe understanding and the implication of acquiring this ability. Thus, we are back to our earlier question as to how we ascribe mental states to children and how children come to ascribe such states to themselves and others. What is special about the understanding of older children and adults when they are capable not only of understanding but also of ascribing understanding to themselves and others?

This preliminary sketch provides an outline for much of what follows. The nature of feelings is examined in Chapter 4, the nature of correctness and truth of concepts in Chapter 5, and the nature of intersubjectivity in Chapter 6. Chapter 7 compares the identity conditions for the feeling of understanding with those for the concept of understanding. Chapter 8 is the pivotal chapter, as it pulls these strands together into an account of what is meant by understanding. Chapter 9 examines the range of expressions that may be referred to by the concept of understanding. The remaining chapters examine my account of understanding with relevant literature in psychology, education, and analytic philosophy.

4 Subjective Mental States
The Feeling of Understanding

> You shall no longer take things at second or third hand, not look through
> the eyes of the dead, nor feed on the spectres in books. You shall not look
> through my eyes either, nor take things from me, you shall listen to all
> sides and filter them for yourself.

—Walt Whitman, *Song of Myself*

Whitman, of course, was the evangelist for first-person subjective
experience. In Chapter 3, I argued that understanding should be seen
as including a subjective feeling, an emotion, and an objective
achievement. Feelings and emotions are characterized as having such
properties as valence, strength, and "content." That content is conferred by an appraisal of the current situation in the light of prior
experience; thus, different appraisals evoke different feelings. I will
refer to the content of a feeling state as an intuition with "identity
conditions" that may be quite different from those for concepts
and beliefs.

Sensations, feelings and emotions, and motivations and interests are biological properties of living organisms; they are real, complex, and at the core of what we say and do. Damasio (1994) pointed
out that feelings are part of bodily perceptual experience that relies on
a major structure of the brain, the amygdala specialized for and
devoted to managing emotional and motivational states that are provoked by events in the world. This emotional system does so through
complex interrelations with both sensory systems and the cerebral
cortex, the centers associated with conscious cognition and sense-
making. Though activated or provoked by external situations, they
are necessarily private and subjective, consciously experienced by

someone. Oatley (1992, p. 22) described the emotion process as a series of stages: event coding, that is, appraisal, significance evaluation, action readiness, and a feeling. He writes, "Emotion is a mental state of readiness based on an evaluation [of a stimulus] and with a specific phenomenological [feeling] tone." Note that the "tone," although often called a feeling, is only one aspect of the feeling state. In a recent review, Scherer & Moors (2019) concluded that feelings are bodily states that are appraisals of situations experienced in terms of valence, pleasantness or unpleasantness, and goal relevance, those appraisals determining such activities as approach, avoidance, or further exploration. As physiological bodily states, they have a phenomenal tone, a tingle, or feeling. These complex emotional states constitute first-person subjective experience.

Although feelings are subjectively experienced and conscious, those conscious mental states can also be objectively "ascribed" to subjects. Ascriptions, unlike the feelings themselves, depend, I argued in Chapter 3, upon the available verbal concepts. Ascribing mental states to oneself is what I mean by introspection. Indeed, self-ascription provides one possible theory of introspection. That is, feeling states are conscious and regulate action, but they are not necessarily available to introspective thought. One of my tasks is to show how feelings and emotions relate to the avowal and ascription of emotions, that is, to our explicitly held beliefs about mental states. As mentioned in Chapter 1, in most accounts of knowledge and its acquisition, there is little mention of the role of feelings beyond ruling them out in our quest for objective knowledge: "Wishes and hopes don't make it so," we say in discounting our emotions. Rather than discounting emotion, I propose to examine how subjective feelings are related to explicit, verbal concepts used in the ascription of those states and, indeed, the experience of those states. I want to do this, as mentioned earlier, without claiming that words are simply names or labels for preexisting things or preexisting concepts.

"What it is like" is Nagel's (1974) description of conscious experience, for what it feels like to be a bat or what it feels like to understand. Anything picked up and appraised by our senses, all first-person subjective experience, may be included in the general category of feelings, although distinctions among them are important for some purposes (Searle, 1983). The appraisal process is critical in providing content to a feeling. Appraisals, on my view, are not to be seen as concepts but rather as subjective states evoked by a stimulus situation in the light of prior experience. This is to endorse the Hinton/ Clark thesis that every situation is processed in the light of accumulated prior experience (Clark, 2013). The situations that the feelings are in response to in light of prior experience provide the "content," a nonconceptual content or intuition. In contrast, concepts allow for introspection and ascription to others of those states. Clearly, one needs the verbal concept "understand" to ascribe understanding. Nevertheless, is it appropriate to ascribe understanding to a child or computer that lacks the concept of understanding? It may depend on what "understanding" means.

Consider the feeling of understanding of an expression in more detail. The feeling of understanding has all the features of any emotion – a bodily state evoked by an appraised situation in terms of readiness for action with a phenomenal tone. The feeling of understanding, I propose, may be identified with the subjective notion of "making sense." As I say elsewhere, it allows one to "go on." However, true understanding is not simply a feeling or an emotion evoked in hearing or reading a sentence or text; understanding must meet an objective normative standard of truth or validity. We may feel we understand, when, in fact, we misunderstand. As we have seen, those standards are monitored by the Turing test for computers and by objective standardized comprehension tests for students. When students or computers meet these objective standards, we as observers may be justified in ascribing or claiming that they understand. Ascriptions, unlike feelings, are true or false. Those objective standards do not make reference to a conscious feeling or to the emotion of understanding, nor to whether or not the system could ascribe understanding to itself.

I examine the truth and validity of ascriptions in more detail in Chapter 5, for the moment is sufficient to notice that some philosophers have justified their discounting of feelings while examining how beliefs and understandings can be ascribed correctly. Davidson (2001, p. 11) argued that feelings are irrelevant to knowledge in that nothing pertaining to truth is gained by distinguishing first- and third-person ascriptions. Understanding is ascribed to self as an avowal, he claims, on the same basis, that is, on the same identity conditions, as it is ascribed to others. Consequently, he feels justified in setting aside feelings while attending to the truth or falsity of the ascription.

Yet subjectively experienced feelings have not been dismissed by all philosophers. Both McGinn (1991) and Strawson (2008) argued that one cannot have a concept without experiencing what the concept is about. That is, one cannot acquire the concept of understanding unless one has or can experience understanding something. McDowell (1994, p. 48) went further claiming that feelings are already conceptual. He denied that "sensation is unstructured, non-conceptual data" and argued that "the content of a perceptual experience is already conceptual." Misak (2013), too, claimed that "experience is always already in the land of the conceptual." Both McDowell and Misak, I suggest, give too much to subjective experience. While granting that subjective states have content, I would argue that the content of a feeling is not conceptual, as it is both private and not true or false; it is an appraisal of a situation in the light of prior experience and attuned to action, not a judgment. Nor is it clear why only some aspects of a complex feeling state find their way into the concept representing that state. Quine's (1960) argument on the indeterminacy of translation suggested the difficulties of going from a situation to a concept. There is, I suggest, a gap between word and thing that cannot be closed by the theory of ostensive learning, learning from examples.

Yet feeling states do have a content. To distinguish the content of a subjective feeling from the conceptual content, McDowell acknowledges that the subjective state given by experience may be better described as an intuition. I translate "intuition" as equivalent to "what it feels like." Strawson (2008), too, suggested that understanding has its own experiential (conscious) character, comparable to that which perception has. In other words, one is capable of experiencing what it feels like to understand something.

In the past decade, there has been renewed interest in the cognitive aspects of subjective experience. Janack (2012) reminded readers of Bruner's early warnings that the cognitive revolution had gone wrong in abandoning the issue of meaning. Bruner (1990) claimed that the cognitive revolution had been "diverted" into technical procedures that could be carried out by computers "at the price of dehumanizing the very concept of mind it had sought to reestablish in psychology" (p. 1). He complained, "Mind in the subjective sense was [treated] either as an epiphenomenon that the computational system outputted under certain conditions, in which case it could not be a cause of anything, or it was just a way that people talked about behavior after it had occurred (also as an output), in which case it was just more behavior: "[Subjective meanings were seen as] an effect rather than a cause" (p. 9). Janack takes Bruner's concerns seriously. Experience has meaning or significance to an organism, both as a matter of survival and as a matter of commitment to reality; these commitments are the priors in terms of which any event is experienced. However, as I shall argue in Chapter 11, Bruner perhaps failed to recognize the disjunction between the subjective states he championed and the objective criteria for mental states championed by both computational theories and theories of ascription.

Critiques by Janack and Bruner reprise Husserl's earlier criticism of the objectivist perspective prominent in Anglo-American philosophy. Husserl claimed that the objective stance with its denial of conscious experience created a "crisis in Western science." He saw that a kind of inhumanity was manifest in overlooking the meaning and significance of first-person subjectivity. Whereas Husserl examined subjectivity, William James (1890/2007) simply took for granted the priority of first-person subjective experience, suggesting that "[i]ntrospective observation is what we have to rely on first and foremost and always. I regard this belief as the most fundamental of all the postulates of psychology" (p. 185). While modern thinkers are suspicious of introspection, few deny the reality of the feelings that James introspected about and that made psychology "the science of mental life" (p. 1).

James was one of the Pragmatists, including Charles Peirce and John Dewey, who developed a distinctively psychological approach to knowledge, based on the priority of subjective mental states. They abandoned the absolutist notion of truth and objectivity, replacing them with the idea that knowledge was a product of human effort and based on experience. Instead of truth, they offered some form of "warranted assertability," what could be taken as true for good reason by human subjects. William James, who defined psychology as the science of mental life, saw "bodily experience" as the basic condition for knowledge (2007/1890, p. 4). Dewey (1976/1902–1903), too, argued that acknowledging the "lived experience" and "felt needs" of children was the route to developing their knowledge and enhancing their inquiry. Green (1996, p. 56) took Dewey's *Art as Experience* as a "paradigmatic account of lived experience as the basis for human knowledge." Art is discovery through making. Sensory experience is the guide to satisfying one's needs. With Janack, I see neglect of subjectivity as one of the limits of ascriptivism.

Locke, of course, had claimed that knowledge derived from experience rather than from innateness or from Divine revelation (Brantley, 1984). But Dewey distinguished his own concept of experience from that of Locke, pointing out that for Locke there was no individual, that is, no first-person subjective experience and no personal agency and no personal belief. Because feelings, needs, and emotions are an essential part of Dewey's theory of inquiry, he was critical of forms of school assessment that evaluated only outcomes. Nonetheless, the apparent objectivity of test results was sufficiently appealing to Behaviorists and to educational policy makers that the Pragmatist child-centered movement became, and continues to be, a critical rather than a defining movement in educational policy, a policy often at variance with the perspective of teachers who almost universally follow Dewey. I return to the educational issue in Chapter 11.

As Janack (2012) showed, philosophy, like psychology, continues to be more Lockean than Deweyan in that it treats experience objectively rather than as lived subjective experience. First-person subjective experience is the inescapable foundation of human knowledge, as she, following Dewey and Bruner, would claim. While necessary, it may not be a sufficient condition for knowledge. If Turing and the Behaviorists are right, it may not even be a necessary condition.

The capacity for subjective feelings is the defining feature of "sentience," a characteristic of those beings that, according to the OED, are "capable of perception and feeling." Feelings are that aspect of consciousness that we share with other animals and pre-linguistic children. All animals avoid pain and adjust responses to conditions of reinforcement. Even the youngest children orient to novelty and quickly "habituate" to recurring patterns of even complex events (Baillargeon, 1986). Feelings, then, are necessarily conscious, and indeed, define sentient consciousness. Behaviors that express feelings invite, but in my view may not warrant, the ascription of belief or understanding. Something comes later with the acquisition of mental concepts that permit ascription.

States of feeling, then, are not the unique property of humans but of all sentient creatures. Chimpanzees experience grief-like feelings as much as humans do. A recent report described the response of a chimpanzee to the death of his companion: "He went into a frenzy of grief ... He began to pull out his hair and wailed. His cries were heard over the entire garden. He dashed himself against the bars of the cage and butted his head upon the hard-wood bottom, and when this burst of grief was ended he poked his head under the straw in one corner and moaned as if his heart would break" (Lepore, 2020). Grief is a complex emotion with precise cognitive contents, including the loss of a valued object. Yet all this is within the range of nonlinguistic animals. While sentient creatures have an abundance of feelings, they lack what "sapient" creatures, human adults, have, namely the ability to form, entertain, and ascribe emotions, beliefs, and reasons. Brandom (1994), from whom I borrow the sentient/sapient distinction, attributed this newfound ability to the possession of a language.

IDENTITY CONDITIONS FOR FEELING STATES

I have distinguished first-order subjectively experienced events from the explicit, linguistically formulated beliefs that make up the concepts of mind. But the problem remains as to how to characterize the content of such pre-linguistic feelings and emotions. Feelings are difficult to explain because, by hypothesis, they are non-propositional. As soon as one names a feeling – say, the pain produced by touching a hot object – it changes its shape to become a belief "I feel a pain," which is true or false, although saying so neither causes nor necessarily reduces the pain. Yet representing the feeling linguistically may alter the feeling as therapists are trained to help patients do.

One difference between a feeling and a belief, then, is language. Some feelings remain difficult to verbalize, that is, we may have feelings that remain inchoate, that is, feelings for which we lack concepts. However, like beliefs, feelings do have a kind of content. The feeling of understanding, for example, is not just a blank emotion but the feeling that one understands something, that it makes sense to me. It is a cognitive emotion. Nevertheless, what is this "content"? We may make this question more precise by asking: What are the identity conditions for a feeling state? Equipped with the list of conditions, we as theorists could ascribe those states even if those experiencing them could not. The move to identity conditions for ascribing states, as mentioned earlier, is usually attributed to Wittgenstein's discussion of "criteria" for identifying states or practices.

The primary identity condition for an emotion is its "content." Lazarus (1999, p. 12) argued that emotional states are subject to how they are appraised, that is, how they are framed by concepts: "cognition and emotion are always intertwined." Schacter and Singer (1962) provided an interesting experimental demonstration of how cognitive appraisals frame emotions. They injected adult human subjects with epinephrine, an arousal-producing drug. When that was delivered in a joyful context, the drug was experienced as producing happiness, but when delivered in a hostile context, it was experienced as anger producing. In neither case was it experienced as arousal per se. Appraisals for adults are based on beliefs as to the cause of the emotion. But what about nonlinguistic creatures who also make appraisals but do so without such concepts? For nonlinguistic creatures, the appraisal is made directly in that any situation is perceived in the light of the history of prior experience. Conceptual creatures consult their lexicon and grammar.

In their review of the current research on emotion, Scherer and Moors (2019) treat emotion in terms of not only discrete categories of emotion such as joy and shame but also as a process. The process is initiated by an appraisal of an event that leads to or arouses action tendencies, physiological preparedness, and a phenomenal tone. The appraisal process includes such dimensions as valuation (desirability), novelty (strangeness), and goal relevance (interest) that are essential to survival and that animal trainers and child psychologists rely on. Sapient linguistic creatures appraise events with an elaborate category system for appraising feelings, for introspecting about them and for ascribing states to themselves and others. Complex emotions such as shame, embarrassment, pride, schadenfreud require a complex set of necessary conditions, essentially a story, to be experienced at all. Developmentally, too, simpler emotions such as joy and sadness, anger and fear appear earlier than more complex, self-conscious emotions such as shame, embarrassment, envy, and empathy that are indexed by the acquisition of personal pronouns (Lewis, 2014; Griffin, 1988). What, then, is the relationship between these experiential states of young children and the ascription of those states by adult observers? As I will argue, the identity conditions for experiencing an emotional state overlap with but are not identical to those for ascribing those states.

EMOTIONAL CONTENT AS INTUITION

A number of theorists have analyzed the cognitions that make up non-propositional content of feeling states. diSessa (1985, p. 100) characterized young children's understanding of physics, epistemology, and psychology as "first-order" intuitive knowledge. Unlike theory-like deductive knowledge, intuitive knowledge is local and contextual and "phenomenological in nature." Johnson (1988), too, suggested that the psychological intuitions of young children must be distinguished from the conceptual beliefs children later acquire with language. Leslie (1987) treated intuitions as mental representations that are later metarepresented as beliefs. In my view, intuitions are not representations. Mental representations, I shall argue, are exclusively linguistically based. No language, no representation. Without language, one is in the domain of feelings, and the challenge is to specify the identity conditions for those feelings, the cognitive aspect of which may be called intuitions. Intuitions have been most carefully analyzed as part of a general theory by Taylor (2016) and Nussbaum (2001), whose views I shall discuss in some detail because they are critical to the proposals on offer.

Charles Taylor (2016, p. 179) took intuitive knowledge, not as a primitive state to be overcome but as the basic mode of human functioning that language is grafted on to. He distinguished the meanings involved in making true statements from "our feelings or what I have called 'meanings.'" By meanings, Taylor referred to concerns or significance, that is, things that we care about, are committed to, and that determine what we experience: "Meanings are felt" (p. 180). These feelings "are something ... we have, and continue to have, an immediate sense, what we might call an 'intuition' it is a felt intuition" (p. 182). He claimed that these feelings are not merely ascribed to the subject but are first-person "meanings for me, values that I recognize and which move me, I have to experience the felt intuition of them" (p. 183). One can attribute these feelings to others only "if I have some sense of what it is like to experience it, to feel it, to have the appropriate felt intuition" (p. 183).

However, as important as intuitions are, they are not true or false, so the problem remains as to the nature of the content of felt intuitions. Taylor claimed that feelings have an intentional object: "love for mom," "fear of dogs," and so forth. However, on my view, feelings are nonconceptual intuitions and not beliefs that are true or false.

Nussbaum (2001), too, proposed that emotions are forms of evaluative judgment that provide intuitions rather than concepts. Her proposal would entitle one to attribute feelings to animals and young children who, indeed, fear dogs, while withholding the attribution of beliefs about those feelings, such as "I fear dogs." Taylor and Nussbaum both insist that feelings make up a large part of our mental life, including the role inarticulate feelings play in innovative thinking; "[j]oy emerges from a vaguely felt difference into a recognizable distinct experience when we find the words" (Taylor, 2016, p. 190) or understand an expression. Gopnik and Meltzoff (1997) described such a state in eighteen-month-old infants, when those infants not only find a hidden object but also realize they "know where to look," a feeling associated with the acquisition of the word "gone."

NORMATIVITY FOR FEELINGS

Both Taylor (2016) and Nussbaum (2001) provided extensive analysis of the relationship between the emotional states of linguistic and nonlinguistic creatures. Both pay particular attention to the features of the appraisal that make up the cognitive component of an emotion and to the relationship between cognitions implicit in feelings and those explicit in language. The appraisal aspect of an emotion is referred to as its "intentional content," a formulation usually restricted to the content of sentences. Were they correct, language would, indeed, have little to contribute. However, both hedge their bets in further describing the intentionality of feeling states as a non-propositional content or as "felt intuitions" rather than as beliefs. Thus, Taylor argued that truth and logic involve "felt intuitions" and not only logical necessity. One's understanding, he suggests, "has to be ratified by a felt intuition before it becomes a new conviction" (p. 199). He suggests that felt intuitions are at the base of all normative judgments, whether for truth, goodness, or beauty. Intrinsic rightness, what "seems right," not only provides a normative standard for truth judgments but also is the source hunches, intuitions, and indeed of most forms of human and nonhuman cognition. Neither Taylor nor Nussbaum deny that linguistic humans, at least on occasion, rely on strict concepts that allow binary truth judgments. However, both argue that the emphasis on truth–falsity leads us to vastly underrate the importance of the subjective feelings that humans share with other animals. Furthermore, they argue that the emphasis on logical concepts hides their grounding in nonlinguistic feelings. Taylor's distinction between the norms for truth judgments and those for feelings is fundamental; those for feelings, I would argue, to borrow a concept from Herbert Simon, are "satisficing," that is useful and believable rather than objectively true or false. Thus, rather than restricting the notion of a norm to truth or correctness, Taylor suggested a second norm or standard for feeling states, that of appropriateness or satisfyingness, what I shall call goodness.

Nussbaum (2001, p. 24, 30–31), too, traced the neglect of emotion in modern theories of cognition to an outdated concept of emotion, namely that emotions are "non-reasoning movements that simply push the person around without being hooked up to the ways in which she perceives or thinks about the world" (p. 24).[1] Once emotions are recognized as having a content based on an appraisal, it follows that emotions are "intelligent," a form of cognition that links a person to a world. Further, she claimed that the object of a feeling is an intentional object, but unlike sentences, "[t]heir aboutness is more internal, and embodies a way of seeing" (p. 27). Finally, emotions are concerned with valuation; "they see their object as invested with value or importance ... to the flourishing of the subject ... to the role it plays in the person's own life"

---

[1] No doubt the Behaviorist assumption that emotion could be reduced to rewards and punishment encouraged this neglect.

(p. 30–31). Emotions have a content that allows assent to the way things are: "What is crucial for an emotion is what the [person] or animal believes, not the truth of the belief" (n. 73, p. 75). That is to say, an emotion is experienced in terms of what the animal or person is committed to, expects, and takes as real. Nonhuman animals and young children "to a greater or lesser extent, lack the capacity to withhold assent from the appearances with which life confronts them" (p. 39). Although Nussbaum shows that emotions have much in common with beliefs, she acknowledges that, where emotions are concerned, "conviction and acceptance, not truth, are what carry the day" (n. 42, p. 46). Nussbaum's emotional states, then, are appraised in terms of their content and their value. Valuation, positive or negative, is a quantitative rather than binary feature that makes it recalcitrant to linguistic representation other than as "intensifiers."

Nussbaum asks the interesting question as to whether or not the unpleasant feeling tone that makes up a part of our experience of grief is a necessary part of emotion. In raising this question, I suggest, she switches from the cognitive content of any experienced emotion to the "identity conditions" for the ascription of an emotion. Note that the identity conditions for the experience of grief are closely aligned to those required for the ascription of grief, with two primary exceptions: preparation for action and the feeling tone per se. This was just the question I raised concerning the subjective and objective aspects of understanding. I suggested, and will examine more fully in Chapter 5, that our subjective experience of understanding is an emotion, with content and a feeling tone. Yet the identity conditions for correct ascription of understanding includes only that content, not the subjective feeling tone. The objective identity conditions for correctly ascribing understanding are completely impersonal and objective and, indeed, provide the definition for the word "understand." Such definitions make no reference to the feeling of understanding. As the identity conditions for ascribing understanding make no reference to feelings, one may be led to ascribe understanding to computers and to children so long as they give the right answers.

Nussbaum (pp. 57–62) makes a similar case for emotions more generally. She asks whether the ascription of an emotion need make reference to the bodily feelings that manifest it. As the appraisal conditions for the emotion of grief, the loss or gain of valued object or goal, already defines the emotion, the feeling "like a knife in the gut" may not be an essential part of the emotion. She offers a hypothetical case of attributing emotions to the gods who, she suggests, may have love or feel sadness even if they lack bodily states. Note the similarity to the case for ascribing intelligence to computers. Both are plausible. Nussbaum suggests we withhold judgment on this question.

In my view, an emotion may be either experienced or ascribed or both. An experienced emotion has a content, that is, an intuition that, in a linguistic creature, may be represented by a concept. The concept, on the other hand, may enter a statement that is true or false and may be ascribed to oneself or others. However, the concept may be ascribed without reference to the feelings. It may be odd to ascribe grief to oneself in the absence of a feeling of grief, but it may not be an impossibility. Jane Austen in *Pride and Prejudice* wrote, "Elizabeth, agitated and confused, rather *knew* that she was happy, than *felt* herself to be so" (1813/1956, p. 278). Elizabeth ascribes happiness to herself in the absence of the feeling.

Taylor, too, insists on the intelligence of the emotions and the continuity across species. Yet he acknowledges that there are differences. The cognitions of linguistic creatures emphasize the true or false statements favored by Aristotle "A is/is not B." The cognitive or emotional states of nonlinguistic creatures are "felt intuitions" and are best represented by metaphor "A is like B" or "A seems like B" or "A reminds me of B" and the like.[2] Behind any utterance is a felt intuition that we struggle to express and feel satisfaction from when we arrive at an apposite expression. To understand something "is to experience it, to feel it, to have the appropriate felt intuition."

---

[2] These connectives show up in student writing, bringing to life the red pencil of the teacher (Turner & Thomas, 2011).

Again, "there is no understanding of what meaningfulness is without a sense of how it feels, the sense that it makes our life worthwhile, that is gives solidity and substance to our biography" (p. 183). Feelings, although essentially human, are not conceptual, as they are not linguistic and part of expressions that are true or false.

Joelle Proust (2014), introduced earlier, can be credited with bringing feelings back into analytical philosophical accounts of mental states. Feelings, she argued, make up a metacognitive system for appraising the products of the conceptual system in terms of confidence, value, satisfaction, appropriateness, and the like.

Proust takes inspiration for her theory of metacognition from John Flavell and his colleagues' work on metamemory, the introspective knowledge of one's memory capabilities and processes involved in self-monitoring (Flavell, Flavell & Green, 1983; see also Schneider, 2008). But whereas Flavell treated metacognition as a kind of knowledge, Proust treats metacognition as a distinctive feeling system that monitors these knowledge states. Conceptual knowledge, typically beliefs, are true or false. Feelings, in contrast, are quantitative and evaluative. She claims that "metacognition is a process that has functional characteristics of its own independent of self-ascription of mental states ... [it exists] to adjust cognitive efforts and goals to one's resources" (p. 4). She makes the interesting suggestion, similar to that of Taylor, that metacognitive feelings also have a "normative structure." While normativity, as I have used it, pertains primarily to truth and falsity, a different normative standard, what may be called "satisficing" or "goodness," may pertain to the subjective feeling of certainty, appropriateness, and value.

Proust's contribution, then, is to add a new dimension to the theory of mind by focusing not only on the concepts of mind but also on the feelings associated with them, including the feeling of knowing, the feeling of remembering, and the feeling of ability. Adults may know how to ascribe knowledge and understanding to themselves or others, but they also have feelings as to the quality of the knowledge, the quality that would allow them to "suggest as possible" as opposed to "assert as true." Such feelings may allow one to adjust cognitive efforts to goals and adjust goals to efforts invested. The feeling that something makes sense is a primary motive for learning, for keeping one at it.

Proust (2014, pp. 122ff.) went on to set out the features of this metacognitive system that are in large part identical to those I have described for emotions. One is that they have a "nonconceptual" content that is attuned to similarities and affordances and suited to adaptive control of behavior. Such awareness and control would be essential for the simplest forms of habituation to a stimulus pattern and all forms of learning and habit formation. It would allow, for example, an inchoate feeling of fear in the presence of dogs, whereas the conceptual system would allow the belief that I or someone is afraid of dogs. Inchoate feelings are what others call intuitions.

Although every subjective experience is unique in that it is tied to unique situations, all experience is in the light of previous experience. Furthermore, there are commonalities that I, following Nussbaum, call identity conditions for feelings. These identity conditions would include content (how the situation that occasioned it is appraised), practicality (attuned to action in its local context), evaluation (desirability and significance), relevance (to specific goals), quantitative (rather than categorical), anticipatory (predictive), associative (rather than logical), qualitative tone (the hum or buzz part of the feeling), and physiological adjustments. Primary among them are three: content, evaluation, and intensity. Together they constitute a felt intuition regulated by the emotional system.

Although feelings and beliefs are related closely, before we can make a detailed comparison of the identity conditions for each, it is necessary to have a more careful account of what is special about concepts and about beliefs. Only then will it become clear that the identity conditions for the two are importantly different. It will also allow us to decide whether and when to ascribe mental states such as understanding to young children, nonlinguistic creatures, and computers.

5 Objective Mental States

Truth in the Ascription of Understanding

Truth is "what is good in the way of belief."
   —Wm. James
The source of the concept of objective truth is
interpersonal communication.
   —Davidson (2001, p. 209)

In Chapter 4, I suggested that young children may experience a feeling of understanding, namely that something makes sense, before they acquire a concept of understanding. However, that subjective feeling may not meet an appropriate level of truth or correctness. Young children may feel they understand, when in fact they misunderstand. Adults recognize the possibility of misunderstanding. Thus, one of the identity conditions for understanding is that of truth or correctness.

This feeling of understanding must eventually be brought into line with the objective standards of correctness. As mentioned in Chapter 2, Kiparsky and Kiparsky (1970) described "understand" as a factive verb that demands correctness, and Sliwa (2015) showed that "understand" shares this factive property with the verb "know." One cannot know something that is false. We, as observers, ascribe or attribute understanding to a person when that person's behavior meets that identity condition for understanding. We self-ascribe when we believe we have met the condition of correctness. Evidence for the correctness of understanding is provided by such measures as answering questions correctly as well as giving reasons and providing evidence. Confidence in our judgment is provided by the feeling that we have, indeed, understood.

The identity conditions for the correct understanding of an expression are precisely those required for the correct ascription of that state. Truth as an identity condition for understanding is met when the structure of an expression is coordinated with the knowledge and goals of the reader to allow the judgment that one knows what an expression means.

A second identity condition for understanding is intersubjectivity. Intersubjectivity implies that understanding is shared or shareable with others. Misunderstanding may be corrected by others. Consequently, understanding is not only a private understanding but also one shared with others. Intersubjectivity is guaranteed by the fact that "understanding" is a word in a shared public language, and, arguably, there is no private language. I consider intersubjectivity more fully in Chapter 6.

As we saw in Chapters 1–4, believing and understanding are not to be confused with the feeling of believing or understanding. This feeling is subjective and quantitative and may be experienced as degrees of certainty and relevance to present or future action. But such feelings are not included in the definition of those concepts. No degree of certainty is equal to the objective criterion of truth. Although the first-person subjective feelings or intuitions of understanding are important, the concept of understanding has distinctive identity conditions that are independent of those felt intuitions. The primary one for the concept of understanding is truth or objectivity.

As we saw in Chapter 4, it is possible that a person monitors their own understanding in terms of feelings of satisfaction, namely that an expression makes sense, while falling short of correctness or truth. Monitoring for truth requires one to meet an objective standard, the standard set by the larger linguistic community, which is often represented by a teacher who decides whether a person (or system) has understood or misunderstood. Once the standard for correctness is known or assumed to be known, one can self-monitor for truth as well as for intersubjectivity.

What determines correctness is not a simple matter. As Kintsch (1998, p. 4) pointed out: "All kinds of elements enter into the comprehension process: perceptions, concepts, ideas, images and emotion. Some of these are prompted by the perceptual system others by memories, knowledge, beliefs, bodily states and goals." Correctness is determined on the basis of not only the linguistic expression but also the beliefs, intentions, and biases of the listener or reader. Kintsch continued: "At the heart of the theory is a specific mechanism that describes how elements from these two sources [text and context] are combined into a stable mental product in the process of comprehension." That is to say, the product is a an understanding that is correct or true. Whether there is a "specific mechanism" that achieves this is open to question. In my view, any rational process is acceptable so long as it meets what can be taken as true or correct.

Behaviorism, like ascriptivism, places judgments of truth in the hands of the ascriber, the authority, rather than in the hands of the subject. This raises the vexed question as to what happens when the subjects themselves become ascribers. I will argue that ascribing calls not only for truth but also for justification of that truth. This comes, I have suggested, with acquisition of the concept of understanding.

TRUTH AND BELIEF

All accounts of understanding language grant a fundamental role to the background knowledge of the subject. The beliefs, values, cognitive maps, and expectancies that make up background knowledge constitute what subjects are committed to as real and true. However, it is important to distinguish the commitments to reality held by nonverbal creatures from the beliefs held by linguistic ones. Linguistic creatures also have these commitments, but, in addition, they have a stock of beliefs that serve as both the preconditions for understanding and the outcomes of understanding.

Whereas psychologists finesse the issue of truth, philosophers of language and mind have long taken truth as a bottom line. Misak (2013, pp. 32–35), in her lucid discussion of the Pragmatist philosophers, defined belief as a cognitive state having content that is true or false, adding, "It is a constitutive norm of belief that a belief is responsive to evidence and argument." She noted that Charles Peirce defined truth in terms of belief, claiming that one "is under a compulsion to believe just what he does believe ... in a manner which he cannot resist." Again, "a belief that is permanently settled is a true belief . . . and to talk of any error in such belief is utterly absurd." Misak criticized Peirce for not sufficiently distinguishing personal subjective commitments – what Peirce called personal truth – from true beliefs that must be justified by evidence and reason. I side with Misak on this matter. That is, commitments to the way things are expected to be must be distinguished from beliefs that are open to judgments of true or false on the basis of evidence or reasons. Young children have commitments; older children have defeasible beliefs. This allows me to argue that emotional states involve commitments to reality even if emotions lack the defining property of beliefs, namely truth or falsity.

TRUTH IN UNDERSTANDING

Judgments of truth played a prominent place in the sentence verification studies pioneered by Wason (1980); Clark and Chase (1972); Clark and Clark (1977); and Carpenter and Just (1975). The paradigm is deceptively simple. Sentences such as "The star is above the plus" are paired with pictures that either confirm or contradict the sentence, and subjects are timed as they make a response. The findings are robust and show that True Affirmative sentences are easiest to verify, while the others – False Affirmatives, False Negatives, and True Negatives – are graded for increasing difficulty. On the one hand, such findings confirmed the notion of grammatical complexity; on the other hand, studies in the same tradition showed the important effects of prior knowledge and expectancies on such judgments (Kuperberg & Jeager, 2016; Olson & Filby, 1972; Wason, 1980). Such studies demonstrated that subjects indeed compared properties of the sentences with those of situations in arriving at their decisions. Such studies show that correct answers not only provided evidence for understanding but also helped to establish the notion that subjects judged their understanding on the basis of the objective criterion of truth. That is, understanding is not just understanding sentences; it is also deciding on the truth of one's beliefs in the light of linguistic evidence.

The verification model, like all comprehension models, glosses over an important part of the problem by translating the picture into a statement that is then compared to the written statement. How one translates the picture into a statement is left unexplained, but the model misleadingly implies that the translation can be done independently of the statement to which it is compared. It is equally likely that the picture is "read" in light of the statement to which it is to be compared. Second, the model seriously underrepresents the complexity of the semantic structure of sentences. Because the sentences are drawn from a well-defined set of sentences, subjects "may discover" the major dimensions – star/plus, T/F, affirmative/negative – and confine interpretation to the features defined by the task. Third, the model downplays the subjective feelings that, as I have argued, may signal understanding to the readers themselves. That is, arriving at the correct answer is assumed to be precisely what it feels like to understand, but these studies make no reference to subjective feelings. Nonetheless, these studies clearly demonstrate that understanding is not merely processing language but also making a judgment, forming a belief taken as true.

Verification experiments, then, carry forward the misleading assumption that the first stage of the comprehension process involves forming a "textual image" of the linguistic expression. This assumption, recall, is borrowed from the hermeneuticists who had warrant for the assumption because they were trying to understand a preserved written text that could be read and reread. But the assumption is misleading in that it gives priority to the text over the knowledge that the reader or listener brings to the text as a set of expectancies, and in that sense is "prior" to the text. Indeed, fervent commitments are not easily turned over by contrary evidence.[1] Gilbert (1991) was the first to point out this bias in the sentence verification model.

---

[1] Former president Trump, along with his followers, refused to change the belief that Trump had won the election even when presented with objective evidence.

Subjects verifying a sentence were assumed to break the verification process into two stages: the first is to "Represent the sentence, represent the picture," and the second is to begin the comparison process that results in a judgment. The bias in the model is that it assumes that the sentence could be "represented" independently of understanding it. Heidegger insisted on the opposite, namely that to represent a sentence is to understand it (Taylor, 2016).

Gilbert (1991) took the claim one step further by explicitly connecting understanding with believing. He asked, "Can mere comprehension occur?" That is, can one understand a proposition without first assuming it to be true, that is, expecting it to be true, to confirm or revise one's expectancies? Here Gilbert's theory coincides with the claim that I attributed to Bertrand Russell, that believing is easier than understanding without believing. Gilbert, however, traced his view to an earlier theorist, Baruch Spinoza, who defended what Gilbert called the Unity Hypothesis. The Unity Hypothesis argues that acceptance is part of comprehension and that grasping the meaning of an expression is believing it. Even when that fails, subjects reevaluate their reading or their presuppositions in an attempt to preserve or update the belief.

Spinoza (1677/1901), in his *Ethics*, allied with Gottfried Leibniz in opposition to John Locke, advanced a view similar to that of Russell. Spinoza criticized the standard assumption that one first understands a proposition and then judges it as true or false. Rather, he claimed that unacceptance is a secondary stage and that comprehending and accepting it as true come together. Spinoza wrote:

> Experience seems to tell us most indisputably that we are able to suspend judgment so as not to assent to things that we perceive . . . (and) that the will, the faculty of assenting, is free, and different from the faculty of understanding . . . (but) I reply by denying that we have free power to suspend judgment. (pp. 101–103)

Gilbert supported Spinoza's view that readers suspend prior beliefs only when problems with confirming beliefs arise. Gilbert (1991) added that "thinkers of all stripes have suggested that doubt is less quickly acquired than belief" (p. 110). He cited as exemplary the research on sentence verification that was mentioned earlier in this chapter. Correct judgments were taken as evidence of comprehension, except that, now, comprehension was to be seen as believing or taking as true.

To a philosopher a sentence may be true; to a living subject a sentence may be believed, that is, taken as true. One of Gilbert's contributions was to show that sentence verification can be converted into the language of belief. When Clark and Trabasso introduced the convention of "setting the default at T" prior to reading the sentence, they were providing an objective criterion for understanding, essentially identifying understanding with belief. Gilbert (1991) took these experiments as confirmation of Spinoza's view that comprehension and believing are one, adding the suggestion that "all sentences are initially coded as true" (p. 113). I would rather say that they are coded as "expected to be true" and that the process continues until one arrives at an acceptable belief.

The success of the early sentence verification experiments came with the realization that one could account for truth judgments by "setting the truth index at True." For the verificationists, this was a convenient way of keeping track of the comparisons made. For Gilbert, and now for me, it was a pivotal insight. The reader comes with an expectation of truth. Mental operations can then be seen as truth preserving. Truth is not only the outcome but also the presupposition with which a sentence is greeted. The resulting belief is taken as the truth, as the way the world is. Carol Feldman (1987) has argued that cognitions always involve a commitment to reality.[2]

In fact, truth as a presupposition for understanding language is explicit in A. Clark's (2013) prediction theory of language processing

---

[2] Carol Feldman was a leader in showing how philosophy could add an important dimension to cognitive developmental psychology and was, for many years, a contributor to our research program.

that he based on Machine Learning. There is an existing cognitive state that is taken as true, and any input is treated in reference to that state, confirming or violating and updating expectations. Kuperberg and Jaeger (2016) have added to the prediction theory by showing that many features of language, from identifying a letter to selecting the meaning of a word, are affected by such expectations. Wolf (2018, n. 29) forwarded this view by claiming that "what we know speeds up the recognition of what we see." Frank Smith (1971) prompted a revolution in reading theory by claiming that reading, too, was based on prediction.[3] It does so, I add, by setting the expectation as confirmatory or true – what makes sense to the reader.

It should be admitted that, although I focus on words and simple expressions, understanding applies to a whole range of speech acts, not only assertive ones (Searle, 1983), and that, with age and experience, readers may be drawn to different forms of texts (Egan, 1997) and different modes of interpretation, including the fourfold meaning of Scripture.

Gilbert's Unity Hypothesis claims that to understand is to believe. But what if one does not believe? Denials reject an expression but do not alter one's belief. Recall Pea's (1980) young subjects who, when shown an orange and asked if it was an apple, replied, "No, orange." They rejected the assertion, preserving their belief. They did not take the interpretive step of entertaining the false assertion as possibly true – perhaps it was a fake apple. This comes later with an understanding of false belief. Adding a new belief on the basis of an expression also preserves truth. Sentences that preserve belief are understood, but in these cases, there is no difference between

---

[3] I acknowledge my indebtedness to my close friend, Frank Smith, who died shortly after I wrote this, for his long-standing advocacy of the importance of prediction and expectation in cognition. Yet this is not a full-throated endorsement of Smith's view of reading. In my view, Smith insufficiently distinguished between the expectancies derived from one's knowledge of the world and those derived from awareness of the properties of one's speech, so-called metalinguistic awareness, and an awareness of the phonological value of the letters of the alphabet as well as the visual identity of morphemes and words. In my view, all are critical to reading.

believing and understanding. Understanding, as distinguishable from believing, arises only when one suspends prior belief in an attempt to construct a new possible belief. Yet it must be admitted that Pea's young subjects understood the question, as they gave the right answer.

Understanding beyond simply believing may yet result in belief, but it would be belief warranted by appeal to the particular properties of the sentence that warrants the revised belief. In understanding, there is a recognition that what the sentence means, what the speaker means by it, and what the listener believes on the basis of it are found to be in agreement. An objective observer would ascribe understanding to a system by showing that not only did the system give a correct response but also the response was justified by reference to the semantic structure of the sentence as well as its context. When subjects apply this same criterion to themselves, they not only understand; they know that they understand. I will later (in Chapter 8) distinguish between understanding with and without the concept of understanding in terms of who is doing the ascription.

Wason (1980) was critical of sentence verification experiments in that they treat negation as a simple variable in a sentence, whereas, he argued, negation serves a particular function in speech, namely for denials of assertions. Russell (1948), whom Wason appealed to in justifying his argument, had written, "If you saw an avenue of beeches with one elm among them, you might say 'that is not a beech.' ... Yet if I see that a buttercup is yellow, I hardly seem to be adding to my knowledge by remarking that it is not blue and not red." Thus, there are no negative facts, only denials of true ones.

Sentence verification, by involving truth judgments, was an important step in bringing truth, and hence belief, into a psychological account of understanding. The second, as mentioned earlier, was when Clark and Chase (1972) saw the necessity of setting the truth index at True even before their subjects read a sentence. Processing involved maintaining or revising the truth index from True to False. Here is Clark and Clark's (1977, p. 110) explanation:

Many people have the intuition that they change their answers very much as the verification model suggests. They start by assuming the sentences to be true, change their answer once on false affirmatives, and false negatives, and change their answer a second time on true negatives. In Wason's experiment, subjects encounter the sentence "The dot isn't blue," when faced with a red dot. People work as if they first set aside the negative and judge the positive supposition "The dot is blue." As this is false, they change their answer to false. But because they had put aside the negative, they must change their answer back to true again. Changing their answer twice takes a great deal of time, and that is why the true negatives take so long to verify.

Young children tend to show the same pattern of responses as adults with one exception, namely that negation of a negation does not necessarily result in an affirmative. Thus, children, in response to a true negative, may "second" or pass on the negative by repeating it as a true assertion. Thus, in response to the true negative "The man has no hat" (in the context of usually having a hat), they may reply, "No, he doesn't," rather than switching to the affirmative "That's true" (Bellugi, 1967, cited by Pea, 1980; Olson & Astington, 2013). Young children seem to have the options of agreeing or disagreeing with expressions based on what they hold to be true, but they are slow to entertain a false sentence as possibly true. They do this later, I suggest, when they pass the false belief task. The presumption of truth is widely acknowledged in the literature (Levine, 2019; Stanovich, 1999).

To summarize, verification models have had two long-lasting and important consequences. First, truth is to be treated not only as a consequence or outcome but also as a presupposition of understanding ("set the index at True"). In this way understanding and truth were brought together; understanding is fixation of belief, not just sentence processing. Second, verification – that is, making a correct judgment – was established as a decisive objective criterion for ascription of understanding to a person or system.

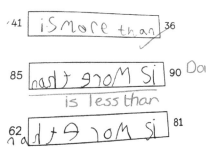

FIGURE 5.1 Which is more?
Source: Courtesy of Sageev Oore.

Language is unique in its capacity for expressing truth. Only sentences with a grammatical structure may be true or false (Bogden, 2009). Thus, beliefs are language-like and, as I shall argue in Chapter 8, entirely language dependent.

The relation between what is presumed as true and one's linguistic resources is nicely demonstrated in a child's attempt to comply with the request to state which of two numbers was larger (see Figure 5.1). Reader, see if you can figure out what the child has done before you read the following analysis.

The problem for the child arises from the conflict between the logical subject, the larger number requested by the task, and the grammatical subject of the sentence to be used in relating the larger to the smaller number. The child resolves the problem by first finding the larger number, what I called the logical subject (the thing to be talked about). Next, the child treats the logical subject as the grammatical subject of the sentence. Consequently, he is forced into completing the sentence by writing backward. In fact, Huttenlocker (1964) had earlier discovered a similar pattern by using fixed and moveable blocks. If the moveable block in the hand of the child is the grammatical subject of a command, for example, "Put the red block (the one in hand) below the blue block (the block affixed to the table)," children find the task easy. Conversely, if the request was to make it so that the fixed block was below the one currently in hand, the task was very difficult. What is in hand, and consequently in mind, even before the sentence is heard, determines how the sentence will be approached and understood. Note, too, the teacher's unsympathetic correction – unsympathetic in that the teacher fails to acknowledge that, for the younger child, "more" and "less" may not yet be consciously defined in terms of each other.

6 Intersubjectivity of Mental States

In this chapter, I return to the second identity condition that, along with correctness, defines understanding. Concepts gain their intersubjectivity, I argue, by virtue of the fact that they are expressed in a public language.

In Chapter 5, I set out the notion of correctness as a condition for understanding. If one understands, one understands correctly. This feature allows a distinction between understanding and misunderstanding. In this chapter, I set out a second feature for understanding, namely that the concept of understanding is applicable to self and the other. In Chapter 2, I pointed out that "understanding" was a word in a public language such as English and, being public, is shared between self and the other.

Wittgenstein (1958) first pointed out the significance of a public language in forming concepts. He claimed that without a public language, there would be no way of establishing correctness for the use of a word, rule, or principle. Rightness can be established only when subject to evaluation by and agreement with others. As the word "understand" is a socially shared expression in a public language, it is applicable to self as well as to others.

Yet it is deceptively simple to posit self–other equivalence as part of the meaning of the word "understand" and to explain the term "understanding" by saying children hear and learn the conventions for the use of a word. Deceptive, for it appears to be a formidable undertaking by a learner to master the self–other equivalence demanded by some words. There is a large literature on egocentrism and perspective-taking largely inspired by Piaget (1962) that shows that indeed children have difficulty in coordinating their own perceptions and expectations with those of other children. Baressi and Moore (1996) explained how children acquire intentional concepts, such as belief and understanding, by learning to coordinate the perspectives of self and the other. Self and other, they suggested, have access to different forms of information; putting them together allows the formation of the concept. Baressi and Moore saw this as a cognitive achievement quite independent of language, "a single representation that can be applied to self and other" (p. 109). Alternatively, it could be argued, following Brown (1956), that the word is an invitation to form the concept and that the "single representation" that is formed is the *sense* of a word.

Although subjective experience is important, there is some question as to whether concepts can arise from experience or from coordinating one's own with others' experience as in perspective-taking. This question is formulated in arguments for and against "ostensive" learning – that is, learning words by pointing to the object the word represents.

Wittgenstein (1958) pointed out that Augustine had a simple view of how words related to things. Augustine said that when he was an infant, his parents pointed to objects, naming them, and so he learned language. One learned a word ostensively, from experience by pointing to its object. Applying this to the concept of understanding, it could be argued that if one experienced the feeling of understanding, one could learn a label for the feeling.

As appealing as the theory of ostensive learning is, it fails for several reasons. First, there is no specific thing that a word like "understanding" points to. A feeling of understanding is a composite of an appraisal, a predisposition for action, and a feeling tone. The thing comes into existence with the concept for the thing as Macnamara (1986) argued.

Bennett (1971), as noted earlier, rejected the notion of ostension. He argued that what Locke and the empiricists called ideas were better seen as meanings. Locke's assumption that ideas are drawn from perceptual experience led him to conclude that a blind man could have no idea of the color purple. Bennett countered that there is no way to tell if a blind man has such an idea other than asking if he knows what the word "purple" means. He may indeed know what the word means even if he cannot imagine or visualize it. Hume (1993), too, tried to get meaning out of experience rather than out of words. The project failed because, in Bennett's words, "a concept or word meaning is nothing like a quasi-sensory mental episode" (p. 353). Thus, he rules out ostension as the way to acquire concepts.

Others agree. Davidson (2001), following Quine (1960), argued that properties of situations are simply incommensurable with properties of words. Beliefs, he claimed, are related to other beliefs, not to properties of experience. In my view, words are connected to experienced situations only in that experiences may serve as the reference of an expression, not its meaning. Rather than words deriving their meanings "ostensively," that is, by pointing to experienced feelings, the feelings provide only the *reference* – not the *sense* – of a concept. The *sense* comes from learning the conventions for the use of a word in the public language, as Wittgenstein argued. Montgomery (2005), too, argued that children cannot learn mental terms such as "belief" and "understanding" ostensively – that is, by pointing to a preexisting mental state; the state comes into existence with the word.

Thus, the alternative to seeing intentional concepts as deriving from coordinating perspectives is to see them as deriving from the senses of words in a public language. Intersubjectivity, an identity criterion for the use of a term, is not the same problem as coordinating the perspectives of self and others. Rather, intersubjectivity comes from learning the sense of a word or expression, that is, the identity conditions for its correct application. So long as self and the other agree in judgment in the application of such words as "think" or "understand," they can be said to possess the concept.

Gopnik and Meltzoff (1997), whose views I consider in more detail in Chapter 10, claimed that this achievement involved the child inventing a "theory." In my view, what is involved is that the child encounters, not invents, a word "think" used by others to which the child assigns a sense applicable to the perspectives of both self and others. In my view, the child cannot invent the concept through reflective abstraction; it is learned as part of a shared language.

However, if meanings of mental terms are not given by sensory experience, how then do they arise? They arise, I argue, when one learns a word, a phonological entity, with a *sense*, essentially a definition, as distinguished from its reference, the statements, or objects referred to. Following Bennett's proposal, I propose to identify concepts with word meanings. This view may be widely shared in analytic philosophy, but it is a radical claim in psychology where concepts are seen as private mental representations and computations in a presumed Representational Theory of Mind.

A more plausible, if preliminary, account would be that understanding is a concept in a public language with phonology, grammar, and a meaning somewhat independent of what the term refers to, namely the expressions understood. McGinn (1991) and Strawson (2008) have argued that one cannot have a concept of a mental state without experiencing what the concept is about. Indeed, there would be no use for the concept of understanding if it did not help to explain the differences between those occasions in which one understands and those in which one does not understand.

My appeal to Frege may require some justification, especially in view of his hostility to psychology. Frege (Dummett, 1993), more than a century ago, dissolved the meaning of an expression into two parts, what he called its *sense* essentially a word definition, and its *reference*, what the word or sentence refers to in a particular context. Frege's well-known example is that "Morning Star" and "Evening Star" both referred to the same thing: the planet Venus. Yet the two expressions have different meanings (*senses*) as shown by the fact that one may know that the Morning Star was Venus but not yet know that the Evening Star was also Venus. To learn that the Morning Star was the Evening Star was a gain in knowledge, not simply learning a synonym. The terms have, as he said, different *senses* (word meanings) but share the same reference. Critically, only words have a *sense* as distinguished from reference; perception makes no such distinction. In itself, this would rule out the possibility that the feeling of understanding was anything like a verbally expressible concept. It would also rule out ostension as an explanation of the origin of mental concepts.

Frege's contribution was to set aside the notion of meaning as too vague for serious science and to insist that only *sense* was relevant to objective knowledge. Furthermore, a word is understood only when one realizes what the concept refers to or is about. Morning Star and Evening Star mean very little without the planet Venus, their common reference. Nonetheless, I take Frege's conclusion that a concept has a *sense* quite independently of its reference. The sense of the word "understanding" is defined by the identity criteria for understanding. Learning to meet these criteria is all that we mean by the concept of understanding. My only reservation about Frege is his complete dismissal of psychology, including the subjective feeling that something makes sense.

Cognitive developmentalists have reasons for being reluctant to grant that concepts may be identified with word meanings. Reducing concepts to word meanings seems to leave behind the rich experiential knowledge and feelings of young children and other nonlinguistic beings. Also, it would seem to minimize the knowledge or experience that children bring to learning a language. Consequently, it is more common to argue that concepts are formed along Piagetian lines by experience and ingenuity. Learning a word is added only for sharing private ideas. However, if the rich experience of infants and other animals is treated as already composed of concepts, beliefs, and mental representations, learning a language would play little role in conceptual development. The alternative is to acknowledge the independent existence of the sense of a word "understand" as part of a linguistic system and treating experience and facts about the world as references of expressions. In other words, it is the word "understand" with a *sense* defined by its identity criteria that constitutes the concept of understanding.

Thus we arrive, if tentatively, at the conclusion to which I have been pointing, namely that a second identity condition (defining feature) for the concept of understanding is its self–other equivalence.

7 Identity Conditions for Feelings and Concepts

All animals experience feelings as they adapt to situations. These feelings clearly resemble beliefs. By comparing the identity conditions of feeling states with those for concepts and beliefs, we may see both why we are tempted to ascribe beliefs and understanding to very young children and computers and why those ascriptions are in some ways misleading.

Feelings are conscious states evoked by situations and, presumably, experienced by all animals. Most of us judge the feelings of young children and other animals as sufficiently similar to our own that we attribute or ascribe feelings, understandings, and beliefs to them. Clearly, the ascription of mental states, a verbal practice, depends on the availability of concepts. The question is whether the states themselves depend on such a verbal practice. I have suggested that they do. Those concepts, represented as the senses of the word "understanding," go beyond feelings to include both correctness (Chapter 5) and intersubjectivity (Chapter 6). Thus, the relationship between subjective feeling and the concepts representing those feelings may be compared in terms of their "identity conditions," that is, the features that distinguish them that came to light in the discussion of the views of Taylor and Nussbaum and Jackendoff (2012).

The identity conditions for feelings and beliefs are further elaborated by Proust (2014), whose views I discussed in Chapter 4, who distinguished cognitive states, such as believing and knowing, from affective states, such as the feeling of knowing and the certainty of beliefs. These feelings, she suggested, serve as a monitoring system for appraising cognitive states, such as belief and understanding. Thus, she postulates two systems, a categorical, analytic system essential for the ascription of beliefs, desires, and intentions, and a subjective feelings system devoted to monitoring those categorical ascriptions in terms of availability, utility, and certainty. As the monitoring system is about the states in the analytic system, it is a metacognitive system. She points out that whereas the system that assigns mental states such as believing and understanding are categorical, linguistic, and propositional, the system that monitors it is nonrepresentational and quantitative. The categorical system is normative in that it allows judgments of truth or correctness. The monitoring system, Proust claims, does not decide on the truth or falsity of the state but it may indicate the degree of certainty, utility, or relevance. These features constitute the identity features that distinguish cognitions and feelings.

Proust claims that the monitoring system is a sui generis system. One of Proust's contributions is to overturn the historic reluctance of analytic philosophers to acknowledge any role for emotion in cognition. However, in my view, metacognition should be recognized not as a system sui generis but as an acknowledgment of the role of emotions, that is, the affective system, in thought as well as in behavior.

Nonetheless, Proust's distinction between cognition and metacognition is fundamental. The former meets the normative condition for truth, the latter does not. Indeed, if we recognize feelings as subjectively experienced, Proust's metacognitive states may be seen as meeting a very different normative condition, what I called, following the lead of Herbert Simon, "satisficing," meeting a practical standard of succeeding, and that allows one to go on. I think of this second normative condition, borrowing from Kant's second critique, as "goodness." Goodness in the broadest sense contrasts with the norm of truth or correctness. We may recall Taylor's (2016) point that when we know something, we are both correct and feel certain.

Once feeling states are distinguished from conceptual states (beliefs), it is possible to compare them in terms of their distinctive identity conditions. The identity conditions for feelings and beliefs differ in at least four fundamental respects. First, they meet contrasting normative conditions. The normative condition for the ascription of states such as believing or understanding is one of truth. That is, ascribing the belief that the child is afraid of dogs or thinks that dogs bite is true or false. On the other hand, the normative condition for the feeling state is that of goodness, that is, the adaptiveness or utility of the state for actions such as approach or avoidance. This latter normative condition is attuned to success or failure rather than truth. Some other contrastive features such as categorical (digital or binary) as opposed to continuous or quantitative are also captured by this second normative condition. Thus, truth, as opposed to adaptiveness, distinguishes concepts from feelings.

Second, feelings and concepts differ in regard to their feeling tone. Clearly, the truth of a belief does not depend on the sincerity with which it is held. Feelings are in part defined by their feeling tone, pleasure, or pain, for example. Even for concepts of emotions such as grief, the feeling tone may be irrelevant. The feeling and the concept of feeling differ in that the latter is linguistic. The feeling tone is intrinsic to the experience but may or may not be part of the identity conditions for the mental state term representing the feeling. To ascribe pain to someone, it is not necessary to feel that pain any more than to ascribe that knowledge is to feel the certainty. Recall Nussbaum discussion of the grief supposedly experienced by angels. The subjective feeling tone, she argued, may not be important to the definition of mental term. Indeed, definitions of mental terms may make no reference to subjective states. The word "grief" does not, necessarily, bring tears or even apply to me. Furthermore, the loss of the subjective feeling is what makes the concept objective, judgeable as true or false and applicable to self and other. Hence, the identity conditions of truth and intersubjectivity are unique to the concepts, not to feelings. That does not mean that the feelings are irrelevant; they constitute a second system, as Proust, Taylor, and Nussbaum argued.

Third, the identity condition for concepts is intersubjective, applicable equally to self and the other. Those for feelings are personally felt and, therefore, egocentric. Proust, to my knowledge, failed to capture the essential intersubjectivity of concepts.

Fourth, the identity conditions for ascription are social, shared in a public language, and makes no appeal to a private language of thought. Because concepts are linguistic objects, they can be avowed as well as ascribed. That is to say, language makes introspection and thought possible.

Fifth, the identity conditions for ascription include feature or features that distinguish the state from related states. Those I proposed distinguish understanding from misunderstanding but may have to be augmented to account for the differences between remembering and understanding, for example, or to distinguish between understanding with and without belief. Hence, identity features beyond truth versus correctness may be involved as well.

Yet the identity conditions for a feeling and the ascription (concept) of a feeling overlap in important respects. We may ascribe fear to a child even if the child lacks the concept of fear. However, it should be clear that it is the ascriber who has the concepts of fear, who knows what fear is and whose ascription is true or false. Although the feeling is not identical to the concept for the five reasons just enumerated, it is sufficiently similar that the feeling may serve as the referent of the concept, what the concept refers to or is about. Similarly, we may ascribe understanding to a child who lacks the concept of understanding. However, in my view, the ascription when applied to child who has the feeling without the belief may invite what I call an "ascription fallacy." Nonverbal subjects have feelings, not beliefs. Similarly, the ascription of understanding to children lacking the concept may or may not be appropriate.

The close, if not identical, conditions for experiencing a feeling, including the feelings of knowing and understanding, to the identity conditions for correct ascription of knowing provides ground for the fruitful interaction between intuition and knowledge discussed by Taylor.

A young child has expectations based on experience that the world is a particular way and feels that a particular course of action is desirable. Taking the world to be a certain way is a felt intuition or a conviction that an adult ascriber may represent as a belief. For the child it may not be a belief but rather a set of expectations, including the feeling that things will go on much as before. But that feeling meets only the normative condition for goodness, that is, for success in prediction and action. It is the ascriber's concept that is true or false, not the child's anticipations and feelings. The verbal concept of understanding employed in ascription may refer to those expectations but only when one acquires the word "understand" with its distinctive *sense* separate from its reference.

Following the lead of emotion theorists, I grant that feelings include the cognitive dimensions conferred by appraisal, as well as their predispositions for action and their phenomenal tone. Appraisals as part of an emotional state look suspiciously like the concepts that we use in ascribing states to them and that, in fact, children acquire when they come to represent feelings conceptually. Feeling fear of loud noise has much in common with the belief that one is afraid of loud noise, the former a feeling, the latter a concept that allows a true–false judgment. The contents of an appraisal, however, are not concepts in that they are not true or false. They are better described as Taylor's intuitions, seemings rather than believings, than they are as concepts or beliefs. These are the feelings we share with our children and with other animals. Concepts allow us to think about feelings and, in the process, turn us into sapient, that is knowing, creatures.

Noteworthy is the fact that the identity conditions for believing or understanding make no reference to neurological or computational processes that are implicated in such processes.

I began the analysis of understanding by contrasting avowals with ascriptions, one based, I assumed, on subjective feelings and the other on meeting objective conditions. In the course of the discussion, it has become clear that one cannot avow or ascribe without verbal, that is, linguistic concepts. Avowal is simply self-ascription. Feelings become introspectable only through acquisition of linguistic concepts, the very concepts used for ascriptions and avowals. Nor does the subjective feeling of understanding define the concept of understanding; an intuition is not a belief. Nor can subjective feelings simply be brought to consciousness to become concepts. Feelings and concepts are distinctive domains. However, they share identity conditions such that feelings may provide a referent for the concept and invite linguistic creatures to ascribe cognitive states to systems that may or may not fully warrant them.

It is not always easy to tell a feeling from a concept. The same quantity poured into a differently shaped container now appears, to a young child, to contain a different amount, as Piaget discovered. That appearance, on my view, is a feeling; one container "seems" to contain more. The concept of quantity that allows the child to override the feeling is, I would argue, a language-based concept, the concept of quantity, and, when learned, is experienced as a personal discovery. In an informal experiment with two of my own, then young, children, I purchased two identical toothbrushes, one pale pink and one pale blue, the blue one for the son, the pink for the daughter! They never confused the toothbrushes. Some days later, I asked them to identify their toothbrushes, which they did, and then I asked which is blue and which is pink. Neither child could answer those questions even if they correctly discriminated the toothbrushes on the basis of just those colors. The concepts of your toothbrush and mine were evoked on the basis of color but without evoking the verbal concepts of pink and blue. Color was an identity feature for the object, without being a lexical concept. Color, here, is what I mean by a nonconceptual content in that it affects behavior. Davidson (2001, p. 124), too, claimed "being able to discriminate cats is not the same thing as having the concept of a cat." Thus, as I said earlier, anything I take away from the child by way of belief, I give back by way of feelings.

ASCRIBING MENTAL STATES

My analysis of feelings and beliefs may allow us to sort out in a preliminary way how mental states such as understanding are ascribed. The four uses of mental terms I have in mind are (1) the ascription of mental states to adult humans, (2) the ascription of mental states to other animals and pre-linguistic children, (3) the ascription of mental states to computers, and (4) the ascription of mental states for oneself. While I have questioned the attribution or ascription of mental states to young children and computers, it is important to explain why we adults continue to ascribe feelings and beliefs to a broad range of entities including brains and computers.

For human adults, the case seems clear. We ascribe the states of believing, thinking, knowing, guessing, and understanding correctly and validly because we share a language for ascription, and we can check our ascriptions against the identity criteria for those ascriptions through further discourse.

But we frequently ascribe those states to characters that are clearly unable to ascribe such states. We ascribe beliefs to young children and other animals because their actions are similar to those of ourselves when we adults act on our beliefs. Our ascriptions are appropriate if their behavior meets the identity conditions for that state even if the child or animal in question lacks the concept of that state. Thus, for understanding, if a child's response meets the criteria of correctness and if that state is mutually recognized, then it would seem appropriate to ascribe understanding to them. Young children failed to distinguish errors from misunderstanding from which I inferred that they lack the concept of understanding.

Ascribing mental states to computers is justified in much the same way. Here we ascribe intelligence or understanding on the basis of the program's ability to achieve outcomes that meet the identity conditions for understanding, namely acting in a way indistinguishable from humans. They do so in passing the Turing test. Furthermore, ML systems appear to meet both of the criteria of correctness and intersubjectivity in that we as adults agree with the decisions made by the computer. In this, the ML system is similar to that of students who pass a comprehension test. It is unclear if the system has the concept of understanding. The test case would be whether the system could ascribe understanding and distinguish understanding from misunderstanding. Unlike young children, as the computer lacks emotions, it presumably lacks the feeling of understanding. But as emotion is independent of correctness, that may not be an impediment to ascribing understanding to computers. Although evidence is lacking it seems clear is that the computer cannot ascribe understanding to itself or others suggesting it lacks the concept of understanding. If so, the computer could not judge that one understood nor could it distinguish understanding from misunderstanding. These, of course, remain conjectures.

Finally, the analysis of identity conditions for feelings as opposed to those for concepts provides some grounds for explaining why feelings are important to the formation of concepts. They do so, not through ostensive learning as I rejected earlier, but by providing a reference for the concept, a feeling of certainty that accompanies successful understanding an expression. The *sense* or meaning of the concept, its identity conditions, are those of the word "understand," a word in a public language. But there is little utility in a word if it lacks reference, that is, if it does not allow distinction between those expressions we feel we understand from those we feel we do not.

8   What "Understanding" Means

Ascribing Understanding

> In this chapter, I explore the difference between having understanding
> ascribed to one, as in the case of young children and computers, and being
> able to ascribe understanding to oneself and other, a capability of older
> children and adults. I call this the "ascribe to" as opposed to "ascribe by"
> distinction. I argue that it is the act of ascription that turns understanding
> into a rational process, subject to reason. More speculatively, I argue that
> self-ascription turns understanding into an introspectable mental state,
> namely something that it is like to understand.

In Chapter 7, I argued that it was appropriate for us to ascribe understanding to young children and computers, as their behavior meets
the criteria of correctness and intersubjectivity. What they cannot yet
do, I argued, is ascribe understanding – that is, claim or attribute
understanding – to themselves or others. Why does that matter?

Here is why words matter. Obviously, one cannot ascribe understanding without knowledge of the concept or the word "understand."
After all, ascribing is a "saying," and one cannot say anything without
using words. Acquisition of the concept of understanding, like that for
any concept, is a matter of learning the identity conditions to be met
for using the word. More important is that ascription is not simply a
description but also a speech act, a claim, or assertion that something
is the case (Derry, 2013, p. 2). A claim about understanding can be
made only if one knows that the conditions for sincerely applying the
concept have been met. In this, ascribing understanding is like
ascribing lying; one cannot ascribe a lie unless one knows the criteria
to be met for the term "lie." In order to ascribe understanding, one
must know the rules for ascribing understanding, that is, know the
conditions for correct ascription. In this, ascribing understanding goes
beyond merely having understanding ascribed to one in that the

criteria have become explicit and known if one is to ascribe understanding.

The initial motivation for making the distinction was to provide an account for the fact we want to say that young children clearly understand expressions (ascribe to) and yet lack the concept of understanding that would allow them to make the ascription (ascribe by) themselves. But the distinction offers a possible explanation of two implications of the distinction. The first is that ascription (ascribe by) requires specific attention to the identity criteria to be met in ascribing understanding. The second is that ascription of understanding to oneself turns understanding into an introspectable mental state. I consider them in turn.

ASCRIPTION AS A RATIONAL NORMATIVE PROCESS

If ascription is recognized as an assertion or claim, it becomes clear that the one making the assertion is responsible for the truth of the claim. If one claims that oneself or another person understands a statement, the speaker is giving their word for the truth of the claim and may be held accountable for it. One may be asked to justify the claim and answer the further question "How do you know?" This is because an assertion is a truth claim that may be justified by evidence and reason. This is why ascribing understanding is a rational process. One must have and be able to provide reasons for the appropriateness of the ascription. Sometimes this will be an appeal to evidence from the expression under consideration, and at other times it may be an appeal to definition: that is what understanding means.

On the other hand, when understanding is ascribed to a young child or a computer, the question of accountability is not raised. We ascribe understanding to a system so long as its behavior meets our standards of correctness; there is no assumption that the system knows the standards, is responsible for meeting them, or would claim any understanding of understanding. Understanding is, so to speak, simply laid on it. Only if they claim to understand do they take on responsibility.

On occasion, a parent or other authority will attempt to make the listening child take on responsibility by asking, "Do you understand?" In such cases, it is often a demand for compliance rather than a request for information about a mental state. However, the attempt to hold the listener accountable for his or her understanding is an important route to helping the learner to take responsibility. One learns to be responsible for oneself by being held accountable by others (Olson, 2007). Taking responsibility is a moral process; it puts one under an obligation.

In order to ascribe understanding, one must know or have reasons to believe that the conditions for correctness and intersubjectivity have been met. Wittgenstein distinguished behavior that can be described by a rule from actions that resulted from deliberately following a rule. His distinction captures much of what I described as the "to" and "by" distinction. To follow a rule, one must know what the rule is. Ascribing understanding – that is, to claim that one understands – is to follow the rules for making appropriate ascriptions. This is to give the ascription of understanding agency and accountability as well as rationality.

There is a considerable literature on rule following in developmental research. Zelazo and Jacques (1996) showed that the ability to follow a rule that violated their habitual response developed at about the same time as other theory of mind tasks. They claim that the ability to follow the rules is a developmental change associated with development of the frontal lobes of the brain.

In this vein, and to anticipate something I consider in more detail in Chapter 11, the ability to ascribe understanding would go some way in explaining both learning to write, that is "composition" and learning to read critically "comprehension monitoring." Both require the self-conscious decision, the self-ascription or judgment that the criteria for understanding an expression have been met. That judgment can be made only if one knows and is aware of the criteria against which writing and reading performance is monitored and the kinds of evidence that may be used to justify the ascription.

As noted, it is the appeal to evidence and reason that makes ascription of understanding a rational practice.

For example, one may claim that another person misunderstood a sentence because it was incomplete, ambiguous, or contained subtle but overlooked grammatical properties, such as a negative or a plural morpheme. Or one could claim that someone did not understand a riddle because he or she did not notice that "flies" can be either a noun or a verb. Ascribing or attributing understanding or misunderstanding calls on and, in that sense, brings awareness to the property of language that provides evidence for the judgment. This is why the concept of understanding – that is, knowledge of how to use the word "understand" – is critical to comprehension monitoring; it brings out the critical features implicit in the *sense* of the word "understand."

In both composition and comprehension monitoring, the ascription of understanding is assumed to be an objective judgment based strictly on meeting explicit criteria. The possible role for the feeling of understanding has not been part of this research.

Ascription is a linguistic practice in the hands of the ascriber. Ascription is essentially a third-person perspective, a view from the outside even when applied to the self. We adults correctly ascribe understanding to children only when we meet the identity conditions for understanding, namely correctness and intersubjectivity. But it is the ascriber who knows these conditions and judges whether someone's understanding has met the criteria. In learning the word "understand," children are acquiring what is needed to become an ascriber.

SELF-ASCRIPTION OF UNDERSTANDING
AS A MENTAL STATE

The ability to ascribe (ascribe by) as opposed to having a mental state ascribed to one (ascribe to) may play a special role in the consciousness of mental states. My suggestion is that the ability to ascribe understanding to oneself is to create an introspectable mental state of understanding. The mental state of understanding is the state of knowing that one has met the conditions for correct ascription of understanding. This may sound circular, but it is not. There is something that it is like to understand. That something is a combination of the knowledge that one has met the criteria for understanding accompanied by the feeling that one truly understands. Recall my "A ha" to the Magritte painting. There is some support for this interdependency between concept and state. Searle (1983) described mental concepts as "causally self-referential," and Hacking (1996) described psychological concepts as having a looping effect, thus both defending the notion that mental concept may depend on the language for representing those states. In my view, the concept creates an introspectable mental state. That state is uniquely tied to the concept.

The importance of ascription, of doing the ascribing rather than being the recipient of an ascription, may be seen in children's acquisition of the concept of belief. Children's newfound ability to predict the action of someone holding a false belief is taken as evidence that the child has learned the concept of belief. But having the concept is nothing other than the ability to ascribe a belief to others. The ability to ascribe, then, is the only evidence that the child now possesses the concept of belief. Moreover, it raises the question of whether children have beliefs before they acquire the ability to ascribe beliefs to themselves and others. We may ascribe beliefs to young children and other animals when their behavior meets our criteria; we make no claim that they know these criteria: these are our criteria, not theirs. The criteria may be met via a feeling or by a computational process without knowing what the criteria for ascription are.

The interdependence of the mental state and the concept of that state may be seen in the case of surprise. Children are easily surprised, but it is not easy for young children to understand surprise or to ascribe surprise to others. The test for understanding surprise is not to surprise children but to see if they can ascribe surprise to others. Can they anticipate how another would feel and react to the conditions we would ordinarily take as defining surprise, namely the violation or expectation of an actively anticipated event? Apparently not until they are six or seven years of age (McLaren, 1990; see also Davidson, 2001, p. 104). It is not only the subjective state, the feeling, that is decisive but rather the conceptual knowledge that would permit one both to experience and ascribe that state. Thus, ascription, a linguistic practice, marks the move from not only feelings to knowledge but also to the mental state of surprise. The mental state does not occur before the concept of that state, that is, before they know the meaning of the word "surprise." It should be acknowledged that children sometimes learn a word before they know its correct use as we saw earlier in young children claiming that they knew when they merely guessed correctly.

Correct behavior may warrant *our* ascription of understanding but be an insufficient basis for ascription of a mental state of understanding. Young children and other animals may meet the first but not the second. The difference, as mentioned earlier, is the ability to ascribe those states to themselves and others. The verbal concept of "belief" is what permits ascription; conversely, ascription is the critical test for the possession of the concept. Ascription requires concepts in a public language; the states themselves exist only in creatures that possess that language. Put another way, only a person with a concept of belief can know that they believe or experience that state as a thought. Knowing what one believes also invokes the feeling of certainty. Together they make up a mental state. Note that none of this makes any appeal to the brain or computational processes that make such practices possible.

The importance of the ability to ascribe, as opposed to having an ascription applied to one, shows up equally well in the ascription of understanding. If children comply, we may ascribe understanding to them. They may still lack the ability to ascribe understanding to themselves and others. The best test for the ascription of belief, as we have seen, is the ability to ascribe false belief. In the same way, the ability to ascribe misunderstanding is, perhaps, the most appropriate test for knowledge of what it means to understand.

We credit children with understanding when they understand an expression correctly and in a way that is agreeable to us. However, a critical shift occurs when they begin to recognize and ascribe misunderstanding to themselves or others. The young children studied by Robinson, Goelman, and Olson (1983; see also Markman, 1981, and Torrance & Olson, 1987) were asked to play a communication game in which one child attempted to convey to another child, separated by a barrier, which one of four blocks, varying on two dimensions, color, and size, they had chosen. Occasionally, a child would produce an ambiguous message, as when one child said "Pick up the red block" when two red blocks, one large and one small, were available. Consequently, the listener occasionally picked up the wrong red block. When communication failed, the younger children blamed the listener for picking up the wrong block. Only the older school-age children blamed the speaker and his or her message: "You didn't say which red block." Thus, the older children recognize misunderstanding by tracing it to some feature of the text in its context. Their concept of understanding is manifest by their ability to ascribe understanding on the basis of evidence rather than by having understanding ascribed to them by adults.

The importance of the ability to ascribe, as opposed to having states ascribed to one, shows up as well in the experience of emotion as opposed to the ascription of emotion. We commonly ascribe complex cognitive emotions to animals and in children. de Waal (1999) has shown that capuchin monkeys are happy to work for a slice of cucumber. If they see that a conspecific, for similar effort, receives a grape, they protest noisily. Their emotional response meets at least some of the identity condition for the concepts of disappointment or injustice, and hence we feel warranted in ascribing such states to them. What they cannot do, I suggest, is ascribe disappointment or injustice to themselves or others. Consequently, they feel no qualms, I suspect, in eating the preferred fruit in the presence of others lacking that food. Ascribing, unlike the feeling, is a form of knowledge that depends upon concepts in a language. Perhaps I underestimate animals, as de Waal claimed most humans do, in that animals do show social feelings such as that we recognize as grief and sympathy. Even then, the feeling state is not the same as the form of knowledge assumed by the ability to ascribe those states.

To return to Nussbaum's earlier discussion of emotion (Chapter 4), both the strong feeling of grief and the concept of grief would seem to include the irrevocable loss of a highly valued object. An animal's strong feelings provoked by the loss of a valued object may be experienced in the absence of the concept of grief. The verbal concept of grief allows an ascription that is true or false and as applicable to self and the other. The concept is a verbal concept, that is, the *sense* of the word "grief." Is the experience of grief experienced differently because of the availability of the concept? I have suggested so. As an animal or a young child lacks language, it cannot ascribe or attribute that state to itself. It cannot know – that is, it cannot hold as true the belief that it is grieving or that someone else is grieving. As they don't understand grief, they may not feel "grief" in the same way that we do. Indeed, they may experience it more deeply; representing the feeling in a concept allows objectifying the feeling.[1] Language users can conceptualize grief in the absence of the feeling, can know that "this is grief" and distinguish grief from mere sadness, distinctions carried in the language.

To review. Introspectable mental states of believing and understanding exist only when one is able to correctly ascribe belief and understanding to oneself and others. Possession of the concept depends on knowing the conditions under which the concept is correctly ascribed. The main identity features for the concept are correctness or truth and intersubjectivity. The identity features for understanding are just those for the word "understand," a word with a phonology, a *sense*, and a reference. Understanding is the ability to use the word to correctly ascribe understanding and

---

[1] Petrarch is reported to have written, "He who can say how he burns, burns little."

misunderstanding. Ascription is an assertion that can be made only when one has some awareness of the criteria to be met and the kinds of evidence required to justify the ascription, a competence put to the test in comprehension monitoring. Finally, self-ascription of understanding creates an introspectable mental state of understanding.

Identifying understanding with the ability to ascribe understanding raises as an important question as to the *ontological* status, that is the existence, of the mental states that the concepts appear to refer to. The concepts in question – belief and understanding – and the states they refer to come into play only in that public language. Without that public language, there would be no belief to ascribe and no understanding to achieve. It appears that it is the ascriptions that populate our minds with mental states; only those capable of ascribing belief and understanding to themselves actually possess the states ascribed. However, words are not only idealized meanings – words also have reference. What mental terms refer to may be rephrased, as Wittgenstein suggested, with the question of how the word is used. Words are used to distinguish those expressions we understand from those we don't understand or misunderstand, as well as those we understand from those we believe, and so on. But I would add that there is a mental state of understanding, that is, the state one is in when one understands correctly and justifiably and with an appropriate degree of certainty. There is something that it feels like to understand.

Mental processes are at the heart of psychological explanation. The psychological studies of understanding language that I reviewed in Chapter 4 show that understanding is an outcome of a set of mental processes that aim at preserving truth rather than, as widely assumed, unconscious computational processes. Similarly, in developmental psychology, it is often argued that children have beliefs and other mental states quite independently of their concepts and words for those states (Perner, Zauner & Sprung, 2005). Indeed, the dominant explanatory framework employed in cognitive psychology is the Representational Theory of Mind (Fodor, 1975) that I discuss more fully in Chapter 10. For the moment, it is sufficient to know that RTM offered a kind of mentalese that both verbal and nonverbal creatures are said to do their thinking in. I am attempting to cast doubt on this option by claiming that representational mental states are the subjective side of the language we use to ascribe those states. That is, mental states are just the subjective side of our self-ascriptions and have no existence independent of language. The mind becomes representational with the acquisition of language(s).

The language for ascribing thought, belief, and understanding is a public language, such as English. In my view, only when children learn the language for ascribing belief and understanding, as they do in the late preschool or early school years, is it correct for us as adults to ascribe a mental state of understanding to them. One understands only when one can correctly self-ascribe! This sounds like word magic and in a sense it is. Words are a new key.

As an aside, I would admit that I labor over the issue of ascription in part because in one sense it is a truism. Everyone would agree, would they not, that ascription is a verbal practice. Mental states such as believing and understanding are ascribed to systems that meet the identity conditions for those states. One of those conditions is the applicability of the concept to self and others. Can one attribute without ascribing? No doubt pre-linguistic children can share experiences, but attributing beliefs to oneself or others requires learning a language for ascribing those states. It is children's ability to ascribe that matters to cognition, not having states ascribed to them.

My claim that having a mental state may be reduced to an ascription of that state would seem to be an overreach. At a minimum, there seems to be no way to distinguish our ability to correctly ascribe understanding from the possession of the concept of understanding and from the cognitive ability to distinguish understanding from misunderstanding. That is, the cognitive ability to distinguish understanding from misunderstanding, the concept of understanding, and the ascription of understanding come down to the same thing. Clearly, young children understand what they hear long before they have a concept of understanding. My solution to this dilemma was to acknowledge that only adults can ascribe understanding to them; we are the ones with the concept and we are the ones with responsibility for the truth of the claim. They, too, will have a mental state of understanding when they acquire the concept that allows them to ascribe understanding and misunderstanding.

WHAT UNDERSTANDING MEANS

We arrive at a possible definition for what understanding is: Understanding is what the word "understanding" means. It is the ability to correctly ascribe understanding to self and others. Knowledge of how to use the word "understand" shifts the reference of understanding from a cognitive process to an ability to use a word or concept correctly in reference to expressions. Thus, I return to the claim offered at the beginning of this chapter, namely that there are basically two issues. First, what "understanding" means and, second, who can ascribe understanding. Adult ascribers, knowing the concept, can apply it to children or computers if we judge that their behavior is usefully explained by the attribution. But we linguistically competent adults can also ascribe understanding to ourselves and others. We do so by applying to ourselves the very criteria we used to attribute understanding to young children and computers. That is, possessed with the concept of understanding, we can judge that we understand by appealing to appropriate linguistic and nonlinguistic evidence. Ascribing understanding, therefore, is a rational practice, a practice subject to reason, and it is something for which we are accountable. Children become just like us when they too learn to ascribe and judge understanding.

The more controversial and somewhat counterintuitive suggestion is that one has a mental state of understanding only if one has a concept of understanding. It becomes plausible if we grant that understanding is a rational process that involves the judgment that one understands and that judgment is made for good reasons. Only older children have this capability. In this way, we could avoid the claim that understanding refers to a mental process that exists independently of our ascriptive practices. In general, having mental states ascribed to one does not confer such states; it is the ability to ascribe those states that confers those states. As Searle (1983) suggested, mental states are the sincerity conditions for ascribing them; no ascription, no mental state.

I must say that it was not obvious that the subject's own linguistic competence – specifically the knowledge of the word "understand" – would explain the development of concepts, let alone in some way create the states that the language referred to. Hence, I labored to defend the idea that concepts, including the concepts of belief and understanding, are the product of the ability to ascribe those states to oneself and others.

Similarly, it may seem to be an overreach to claim that the notion of "concept" can be replaced by the Fregean *sense* of a word or expression. Indeed, Brandom (2009, p. 6) asserted that "grasping a concept is mastering the use of a word." The reduction of concepts to word meanings follows from the fact that only words have a *sense* as distinguished from reference. It is the *senses* of words that make up the semantic structures of the language. Hence, words in a language produce conceptual structures unavailable to nonlinguistic creatures.

The linguistic view on offer contrasts with the alternative view that pre-linguistic creatures have beliefs but simply lack the concept of belief, and with the view that young children invent concepts through reflective abstraction for themselves rather than through acquiring them by learning a public language. My denial, that young children and other animals have beliefs prior to having the concept of belief and the ability to ascribe belief, finds an ally in Davidson (2001), who has argued that there are no beliefs without a concept of belief. He justified his claim by pointing out that beliefs are true or false. Without a language that permits true–false distinction, cognitions are not beliefs. I defended the view by arguing that concepts have identity conditions that feeling states lack, primarily truth and intersubjectivity, and that concepts are nothing more than the meanings of the words we use for ascription.

Children's early cognitive processes *are like* beliefs and *like* understanding rather than actual beliefs or understandings that are open to reasons. Similarly, the feelings experienced by young children *are like* those represented by linguistic concepts but are not to be identified with them. Nonetheless, the words we use for ascription of mental states may refer to a feeling of knowing or a feeling of understanding. But it is the sense of the word, not the feeling, that allows one to both ascribe mental states and to draw logical inferences from them.

I return to the basic question as to what we mean by understanding. The word "understand" best expresses the concept of understanding, and, as I have argued, it is a linguistic concept. But there are many suitable, if less precise, terms for expressing the concept, including the somewhat halfway concept "making sense" that I examine in more detail in Chapter 10. Wittgenstein (1953, p. 155) has provided some useful ones: "He understands, he knows how to go on" but he also adds as synonyms "Now I know" (151), "clear view of" (125), "how to go on" (155), "occurs to me" (154). Davidson (2001), too, put less emphasis on particular words than on a more general competence with language or, as I would put it, finding or making a place in the language for a new concept. I did just this when I characterized understanding as grasping a meaning without necessarily believing it. The specific words used may be less important than the availability of synonyms, paraphrases, and circumlocutions for the concept. In sum, knowing the identity conditions to be met for correctly ascribing understanding to oneself is what we mean by understanding.

Wittgenstein raised suspicions about mental processes. He asked rhetorically, "'Understanding a word': a state. But a *mental* state?" (151a, also 154). Again, "Try not to think of understanding as a 'mental process' at all. For that is the expression which confuses you. [Although] there are mental processes which are characteristic of understanding, understanding is not a mental process." In my view, understanding is the ability to correctly ascribe understanding to oneself and others, and the ability to ascribe depends upon knowledge of the meaning of the word "understand." The mental state, insofar as it is a state, is the introspectable subjective feeling that arises when one successfully meets the conditions for correct understanding.

This is, at least for me, to plow new ground. One would ascribe understanding to a person or system if that system met the criteria for the use of the term "understanding." Just what those criteria are has been central to my inquiry. Furthermore, in order to ascribe understanding to oneself or another, one is making a judgment that the understanding is correct and valid, that the ascription is made for good reasons. These reasons include an awareness of the evidence that justifies the ascription. Having understanding ascribed to one, as in the case of young children, is something we do for reasons, but we make no claim that they understand for good reasons. Reasons come with ascribing. If having reasons is included as an identity criterion for understanding, then ascription to young children or to computers is perhaps not justified.

Understanding may be correctly ascribed on many grounds depending on the evidence used to arrive at truth and the standards for interpretation held within a linguistic or textual community. The basic criteria for correct ascription – truth and intersubjectivity – appear to be universal, but what counts as true and who is included in the community that monitors those standards change with the goals and expectancies of the reader, with his or her stage of development, and with the history of reading.

I may schematically represent the aforementioned argument in Table 8.1.

First, the feeling of understanding, the feeling that a situation or expression makes sense, confirms one's beliefs and gives one the confidence to go on. Such feelings may occur both when the standards for correct understanding are met and when they are assumed to have

Table 8.1. *Understanding*

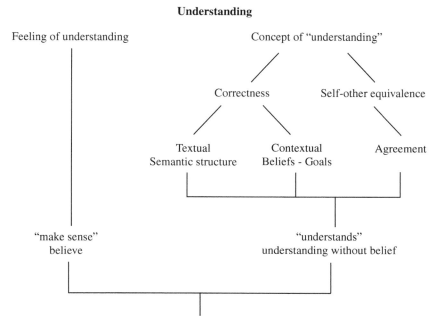

been met so feelings do not define understanding. The concept of understanding, on the other hand, is the lexical meaning, that is, the Fregean *sense* of the term "understand" with at least two identity conditions, truth and intersubjectivity. Truth is justified by relating the text to its context, while intersubjectivity is justified by gaining agreement with real or imagined others. To possess the concept of understanding is just to know how to use, that is, how to ascribe the term "understand" to oneself or others.

That is my account of what is meant by understanding.

9 The Referential Scope of Understanding

The concept of understanding, I argued in Chapter 8, was the sense or meaning of the term "understand." In this chapter, I examine the domain or scope of the expressions that we may understand, that is, the things that the word "understand" may refer to.

It is not surprising that young children sometimes misunderstand expressions. There is a well-known children's game called "Simon Says." The parent or teacher gives the rule: Only do what Simon says. The adult then says, "Simon says touch your nose," but sometimes says only "Shake your head." Children are to comply with the first but not the second. Google provides a brief video as part of its entry for "Simon Says." It reveals, what is often reported, three- or four-year-olds often comply with both, while slightly older children are more able to make the distinction, but all children love the game. The game is an early introduction to the rules for correct understanding. Understanding correctly is difficult because the main clause determines how the other clause is to be understood.

More systematic research demonstrates a similar pattern. deVilliers (2005) told children a story that included the following: "The Mom said she bought apples, but look, she really bought oranges." She then asked the children, "What did the Mom say she bought?" Three-year-old children said "oranges," while the four-year-old said "apples." Younger children's understanding fails to meet the criterion for understanding, but clearly they did not merely misunderstand; they presumably felt that they understood: their understanding, however, was limited to what made sense to them. They understood what they could believe and neglected the rest.

To this point I have focused attention on correctness as one of the features of the *sense* or meaning of the word "understand" and on what is implied by ascribing understanding. I relied on Frege's dissolving the concept of meaning into two parts: the *sense* or meaning of the term as defined by its identity conditions and the reference of the term, that is, its range of application. The expressions "the morning star" and "the evening star" have different senses, but both refer to the planet Venus. Without a reference, there would be little use for the sense or meaning of expressions. So what is the "Venus" that is picked out by the sense of the word "understand"? In other words, what is the range of events that one may understand?

What "understanding" refers to is the mental state that results from the judgment that one's response to an expression meets the criteria for understanding, namely correctness and intersubjectivity. Correctness depends on the appropriate use of textual and contextual evidence. The criterion of intersubjectivity marks agreement but also implies a degree of relativity, namely that understanding is anything that participants in a speech community can agree on.

Any expression may be understood or misunderstood. But it may be possible to distinguish the range of expressions that a child, lacking the concept, can understand from expressions that may depend on possession of the concept. This contrast is highly artificial in that the primary determinant of understanding, I have argued, is prior belief and expectancies, so setting them aside in a task may be misleading.

The question, then, is whether the range of expressions that can be understood changes when children acquire the ability to ascribe understanding to themselves and others. Recall that the feeling of understanding may not distinguish these two categories. Young children may feel that they understand as long as they can recover a possible belief, as we saw previously. But the concept of understanding may be essential to understanding expressions that require them to understand expressions that they cannot simply

Table 9.1. *Understanding expressions*

Type 1	Type 2
Without the concept	With the concept
Feeling of understanding	Concept of understanding
Assigned by others	Assigned by self
Tied to believing	Understanding without belief
Grounds remain implicit	Reasons for justifying understanding
Appeals to truth	Appeals to validity
Ascribed to	Ascribed by

believe. This is to highlight Russel's suggestion that understanding with belief is easy, while understanding without necessarily believing or entertaining possible beliefs is difficult.

We may contrast expressions as two types as in Table 9.1.

Language learning implies understanding. We adults ascribe understanding to them when their response to an expression meets the criteria of correctness and intersubjectivity. They meet these criteria primarily when the expression is sufficiently congruent with context and prior beliefs. In this case, their understanding is identical to believing or denying; conversely, they cannot understand what they cannot believe. Intersubjectivity is met by nods of agreement from another person and a willingness to go on. In most cases, talk proceeds if the criteria for understanding are met.

Acquisition of the concept of understanding is obviously necessary for the ascription of understanding. Equipped with the concept, children can ascribe both understanding and misunderstanding to ordinary as well as misleading statements. Equipped with a concept of understanding, one could, for example, say to oneself, "I thought I understood, but I realize now that I didn't" or "I thought you meant the red shoes when you said 'shoes.'" We may distinguish two classes of expressions: one that may be understood without any special knowledge of the concept or the ability to ascribe understanding, and the other that consists of expressions that arguably can be understood

Table 9.2. *Classes of expressions contingent on possession of the concept*

Type 1 (without the concept) - understanding communication and believable speech acts	
Type 2 (with the concept)	
-ascribing misunderstanding	-understanding false belief
-jokes and riddles	-lexical ambiguities
-syntactic ambiguities	-referential ambiguities
-believing vs. understanding	-literal vs. metaphor meaning
-serious vs. ironic usage	-saying vs. lying
-stating vs. implying	-saying vs. promising
-monitoring, repairing, editing	-written composition
-said vs. paraphrase, gist, summary etc.	

only when one possesses the concept. This class is identical to that described as understanding without necessarily believing. These classes are set out in Table 9.2.

Those of Type 2 require ascription of understanding somewhat independently of what one believes, and one must justify the ascription by appeal to linguistic evidence.

We correctly ascribe understanding of ordinary speech acts to young children if their understanding meets the criteria of correctness and mutuality. However, they appear to meet the criterion of correctness only so long as they are not required to understand expressions that they cannot believe, the insight I attributed to Russell. Moreover, as I argued, they cannot ascribe understanding to themselves; they do not know they understand even if they may feel that they do or do not understand.

What is general across the broad range of cases of Type 2 is that they all pose a special challenge to language understanding; one must become aware of possible meanings. Possible meanings, of course, are those entertained without believing. If an expression cannot be simply believed or denied, children are forced to base their judgment by appeal to the identity conditions for understanding. If an expression meets these conditions, whether it is believed or not, it will be accepted as understood. Such expressions require a kind of double take as in the case of Magritte's famous painting. Furthermore, understanding such expressions make their first appearance about the time children enter school. Indeed, schooling, with its focus on reading and writing, appears to be the primary incentive or occasion for the acquisition of many such distinctions. The concept of understanding is one among the set of concepts that make up with children's "theory of mind" and with an increasing consciousness of language (Olson, 2016).

Understanding false belief is a critical case in that to understand that someone, self or other, could entertain a statement known to be false. That is, it involves the suspension of disbelief. In the false belief task, it is the ascriber who entertains the false belief; the subject to whom it is ascribed need not know that his or her belief is false. Again, this is a case of understanding an expression without necessarily believing it.

Many of these distinctions have been studied in their own right. In the psycholinguistic study of lexical acquisition of quantifiers "some" and "all," Papafragou and Musolino (2003) found that young children accept, while adults reject, the statement "Some elephants have trunks." Very young children accept the expression, as it is believable, that is, not obviously false. Adults, on the other hand, detect the possible ambiguity, pointing out the fact that "some" implies "not all" and so reject the statement. Adults then go on to "repair" the expression by saying "All elephants have trunks." The converse also holds. Beal (1990) found that young subjects are likely to report that a story had stated a causal relation that older subjects admit they had inferred. Hence, what is involved is not the ability to make inferences but rather to recognize when inferences are entailed as opposed to implied by what is said and use that as a basis for ascribing misunderstanding and for revising the expression.

Syntactic ambiguity has been brought into prominence by Chomsky's famous examples: "Flying planes can be dangerous" – the ambiguity here hangs on whether "flying" is an adjective or a verb. In an appropriate context, one may fail to spot the ambiguity in such expressions; spotting the ambiguity requires attention to the grammar. It is recognizing the ambiguity that is late to develop.

Many of the tasks that call for the more sophisticated judgments of understanding require what I called the say–mean distinction (Olson, 1994). The say–mean distinction is analogous to, and acquired at about the same time as the appearance–reality distinction (Flavell, Flavell & Green, 1983). In all the linguistic cases involving understanding, it is important that subjects distinguish aspects of linguistic form from their beliefs. The "say" side of the equation is the semantic structure or "sentence meaning," that is, the "very words" involved in repeating the expression. The "means" part of the equation are the expectancies or predispositions in terms of which the linguistic form is perceived and understood by someone. Problems arise, as Russell put it, when understanding demands more than simply believing or denying to entertaining possible beliefs. This may arise either because the listener holds inappropriate expectancies (beliefs and goals) or because of ambiguities in the expression. Lexical ambiguity best exemplifies the gap. Elizabeth Lee (1995) presented young children with riddles that played on such ambiguities as "flies" as insects versus "flies" as a verb of locomotion. Although children under six years of age knew both meanings, they could not grasp the riddle or consider it funny.

All judgments involving ambiguity require a degree of linguistic awareness. Linguistic awareness is knowledge *about* language as opposed to knowledge *of* a language (Olson & Oatley, 2014). What is critical to the say–mean distinction is a kind of linguistic awareness, an ability to point to or single out the misleading word or words in the expression that may result in misinterpretation. Recall the Robinson, Goelman and Olson (1983) study of understanding that pivoted on referential ambiguity[1], a communicative expression that failed to

---

[1] Linguists treat referential ambiguity as a pragmatic as opposed to a semantic problem.

distinguish possible referent objects. The children who could ascribe understanding or misunderstanding could provide a linguistic reason for the judgment. To repeat, it is not that young children do not know what was said and what was meant; what they lack is the ability to see a discrepancy and use one to "repair" the other. Lee, Torrance and Olson (2001) found, for example, that in prose expressions, children could not distinguish what was said from a true paraphrase. In poetic expressions, on the other hand, they could not accept a paraphrase as what had been said. This reflects the linguistic fact that "said" is ambiguous between direct and indirect speech. "Said" may refer either to the expression or the intention: he said "I'll come" versus "He said he would come." To recognize ambiguity is to suspend disbelief and consider alternative interpretations.

Understanding figures of speech such as metaphor, allegory, and irony also involve understanding without believing. They require that one consider the possible meanings of an expression without necessarily believing either possible meaning. Philosophers have long recognized that metaphor required special interpretation. Augustine (1958, p. 84) claimed that understanding "distinguishes us from beasts" and he took as exemplary the ability to see the "spiritual" meanings of literal expressions. Metaphor required that one "raise the eye of the mind above things that are corporal and drink in eternal light," he wrote. Truth in metaphor may strike a modern reader as premodern, yet we routinely think of our theories and models as true even if they too are metaphors. Winner (1988) showed that young children begin to understand metaphor and irony beginning in the early school years.

Comprehension monitoring research, to be examined more carefully in Chapter 11, explores the limitations of student understanding texts. Comprehension monitoring is a measure of a student's ability to ascribe understanding, which is to judge whether any interpretation has met the criteria for correctness and intersubjectivity. One can ascribe understanding only when one is satisfied that the criteria for understanding have been met. Such tasks assume that children possess the concept and have to learn to justify their interpretation by appeal to evidence. Such activities are useful for teaching students to be more critical readers. The processes involved in monitoring involve finding the source of a possible misinterpretation and repairing the text in such a way that a correct understanding could result.

When understanding is seen as fixation of belief, it becomes obvious that prior knowledge and beliefs determine how an expression is understood. Levesque's (2017) argument for the importance of background knowledge, what he called "common sense," in AI models of language processing, led him to propose a new standard for the "Turing test." As mentioned earlier, the Turing test is the commonly accepted standard (within cognitive science circles) for deciding whether computers understand language. He proposed that the computer be asked questions that one could not answer by closer scrutiny of the text but require one to go beyond the text to one's conventional knowledge of the world. His example: "The trophy would not fit in the brown suitcase because it was too small. What was too small?" There is nothing in the meaning of either the trophy or the suitcase that indicates their relative sizes. He suggested that if such questions were included in the Turing test, traditional AI computers would fail, demonstrating one, perhaps ineliminable, limitation of computer understanding. However, it would be premature to either suggest or deny that "deep learning" algorithms would allow a computer to pass Levesque's test. It is possible that the semantic structures captured through "deep learning" of language include relations between containers and contained as well as the representations of individual words and sentences.

Understanding may be less a problem with evidence from the semantic structure of the sentence than with prior knowledge of the world of literature. Consider G. K. Chesterton's celebrated poem "The Donkey." In the poem, the donkey chides the reader for thinking that donkeys are at the bottom rank of animals:

> Fools! For I also had my hour—
> One far fierce hour and sweet:
> There was a shout around my head
> And palms about my feet.

A reader perhaps grasps that this is something about a donkey on a good day but may be lost as to the possible intent or point of the poem. One looks back at the text in vain; rather one must appeal to what others may know or think, in this case a somewhat obscure piece of knowledge, namely Christ's ride on a donkey into Jerusalem on Palm Sunday. Only when the text meets both the truth and its acceptability to the larger language community does one understand what the poem refers to. While it is conceivable that a computer could detect the incompatibility between "less" and "most" in the previous example, the lack of relevant knowledge would limit interpretation in the second case. Humans, all amateur hermeneuticists, may entertain many possible solutions before arriving at one that could be taken as true.

THE LITERATE BIAS

The appeal to specific aspects of linguistic form in understanding complex expressions and texts goes some distance to explaining why schooling and literacy play such an important role in this development. Learning to read and write involves, as both cause and consequence, an awareness of linguistic form, including phonological awareness, word awareness, and sentence awareness (Olson, 2016). Recognition of the close relationship between these somewhat specialized uses of language and an acquaintance with written literature justified the distinction, sometimes overdrawn, between speech and writing, between oral and written societies, and between orality and literacy as forms of specialized competence (Ong, 1982) and the evolution of specialized "textual communities" (Stock, 1983).

In speaking and listening, the "very words" of a prosaic expression are ephemeral, quickly lost, in the attempt to follow an argument. A written text, to one who knows how to read, provides evidence that can be scanned and reread to recover "the very words" that distinguish between understanding and misunderstanding. In an earlier work (Olson, 1994), I pointed out schooling was, in large part, a matter of learning to pay attention to the very words appropriate to an interpretation of an expression and in composing a written text, both of which require appropriate choices at the lexical, grammatical, and discourse levels.

The close link between literacy, language awareness, the ability to recognize the possibility of misunderstanding is nicely demonstrated in the study mentioned earlier by Norbert Francis (2019). He examined the relationship between language and literacy in a study conducted on Mexican bilingual students learning to read and write both traditional Nahuatl and modern Spanish texts. He reported that the students who scored higher on a test of metalinguistic awareness were able to revise what they had written at the discourse, lexical, and phonological levels. They did so by substituting as subject of a sentence a noun that added to the coherence of the discourse ("deer" instead of "rabbit"), a more precise conjunction ("but" for "and") and a more correct grammatical verb ending ("pareciera" for "parecian"). Those with less linguistic awareness were less likely to make revisions and corrections.

What one sees or hears in an expression, then, depends not only on the linguistic form of the expression and on one's prior knowledge and beliefs but also on the knowledge of the concept of "understand" and its identity features of correctness and intersubjectivity.

10 Understanding and Children's Theory of Mind

In Chapters 8 and 9, I summarized my account of what it means to understand and the domains to which the concept applies. Understanding is the ability to meet the truth and intersubjective criteria for correct ascription of understanding to oneself or others. Understanding, that is, learning the sense of the word "understand" with its identity criteria is sufficient for ascribing understanding. In this chapter, I examine this account in the light of several related or contrasting accounts of mental states, including understanding, and the role of language in their formation.

A philosophical tradition going back to Descartes assumed that human beings have an indubitable consciousness of their own minds but that knowledge of other minds was at best inferred. What they failed to see was that the consciousness, the felt experience that could not be doubted, was not the same as introspection. William James, as mentioned in Chapter 4, was guilty of this conflation. Introspection is enabled by mental concepts used in ascribing mental states to others. Put simply, introspection is self-ascription; one cannot introspect without linguistic concepts of mind. As Montgomery (2005, p. 120) pointed out in regard to children's acquisition of theory of mind, "introspective knowledge [plays a much smaller role] in mental concept formation than is sometimes claimed." Montgomery's concern has been ignored by those influenced by Simulation Theory.

SIMULATION THEORY

Goldman and Shanton (2010) offer an account of what they call mind reading. Mind reading extends the tradition in philosophy that treated mind reading as a problem of other's minds. They advance a "Simulation Theory" according to which third-person mind reading involves the projection of one's own mental states onto third-person targets. This assumes two things, one that the ascriber has conscious access to his own mental states and, two, that it should be easier to ascribe mental states to oneself than to others. Neither assumption is warranted for both theoretical and empirical reasons.

First, the empirical. Gopnik and Astington (1988; see also Astington and Gopnik, 1988) showed that children who could not attribute false beliefs to others could not attribute them to themselves either; there is no first-person advantage. That is, if children cannot ascribe, they cannot introspect. Hence, there is nothing to project to other minds. Second, ascription requires concepts, as Astington and I (Olson & Astington, 1986) have argued, and these concepts, expressed in an ordinary language, are objective, that is, applicable equally to self and other. Hence, there is no ground for granting Goldman and Shanton's claim that one understands another's mind on the basis of something one knows about one's own mind. One knows nothing about one's subjective experience without concepts.

Nonetheless, Goldman and Shanton's Ascription Theory is important for the prominence it assigns to first-person subjectivity. There is, indeed, something that it is like to understand. Feelings provide a reference for concepts. However, those authors conflate one's subjective–affective states with the introspective awareness of those states. As I argued, those subjective experiential states may be necessary but not sufficient conditions for acquisition of the concepts needed for reflecting on or introspecting those states. It is the concept that makes the state ascribable to self and other.

THE THEORY THEORY

The Goldman and Shanton argument is directed against the so-called theory theory of Gopnik and Meltzoff (1997), the central claim of which is that young children are little theorists who build knowledge by advancing possible theories and evaluating them against evidence. The theory theory is an outgrowth of the Representational Theory of

Mind (RTM) widely adopted in the cognitive sciences that assumes that behavior is a product of mental representations and mental operations on those representations in a way similar to standard AI. The theory theory treats mental representations as concepts that are organized into systems that allow for hypotheses and inferences. That young children's cognitions are best seen as theory construction is at best controversial (Erneling, 2010; Apperly, 2008).

How could one tell if young children were advancing and testing theories? Consider Misak's account of theoretical inference, what Peirce called abduction. As Misak pointed out, "regularities abound, but only some of them want explanations. Only unexpected or surprising irregularities make a demand on us to make an inference to the best explanation" (p. 49). This would involve formulating a hypothesis. As Misak put it:

(1) A surprising fact C occurs.
(2) But if A were true, C would be unsurprising.
(3) So possibly A is true and worth entertaining.

The point to note is that (2) is a genuine case of understanding without believing in that it requires that one entertain the meaning of an expression that is purely hypothetical, that is, entertained rather than simply believed. Consequently, (2) is thinking theoretically. However, Apperly (2008) provided evidence that such thinking is not characteristic of young children's cognition but rather depends on the possession of a concept of mind. Apperly goes on to suggest that the contrast between mind reading and theory theory has run its course and it is time to look elsewhere.

Yet something similar to abduction does occur in the practical reasoning of young children and in other animals when they, as Piaget said, substitute means in achieving ends. Kohler's chimpanzee appeared to reason: *I want a banana. I cannot reach it. If I stood on something, I could reach it.* So he fetched something to stand on. Similar "reasoning" is observed in many animals. But note that these are practical reasonings rather than the linguistically formulated ones that we would describe as deduction or logical inference. Practical actions are judged by success rather than truth or necessity.

On the other hand, Gopnik and Meltzoff defend the more specific claim that children acquire some understanding of their own and other's minds through the acquisition of concepts, including the concepts of "believe," "pretend," "remember," and "understand," and raise the possibility that these concepts are essentially linguistic ones. Their research on the relationship between cognitive and semantic development is extremely important. All developmental accounts of children's minds acknowledge an interaction between concepts and language, but Gopnik and Meltzoff provided evidence to show that "learning the word and learning the concept go hand in hand" (p. 194). They showed that young children's understanding of object permanence, namely their search for serially displaced objects, is tied to their acquisition and use of the concept "gone." Further, they provided some evidence that the understanding of means–end relationship is accompanied by acquiring the expression "oh, oh." They argued that the systematic categorization of objects comes in conjunction with seeking names for objects. They concluded that young children's concepts are "related to and reflected in early semantic development" (p. 49).

Gopnik and Meltzoff's account of the seamless relationship between cognitive development and linguistic development is just what is required to explain the shift from practical, experiential feelings into linguistic semantic knowledge. For it is language, I argued, that is the gateway to formulating statements that may be true or false and shared between speakers. And it is language that later permits the formulation of theories. Pre-linguistic cognitive–affective states regulate action in terms of success of failure, but those states, I argued, are not held as true or false. Only linguistic concepts are both shared and possibly true or false. So although "seamless," the move from concepts to meanings is, in my view, a gigantic step in cognitive development. What the children acquire are words and expressions in a public, shared language. Acquiring concepts is in fact acquiring the meanings, the *sense*, of words and expressions. Conceptual development, I argue, is semantic development, that part of cognition that distinguishes human from animal intelligence.

As we saw earlier, there is a partial match between the identity conditions for young children's cognitively appraised feeling states, say, expecting a hidden object to reappear as in "peekaboo" and the identity conditions described by Gopnik and Meltzoff for their later acquisition of the term "gone." This similarity is what invites parents and psychologists to ascribe the concept to toddlers even before they learn language. However, only when infants learn the linguistic form for their subjective state do they arrive at a concept that may be used for description, ascription, and introspection.

The ascription view resolves the supposed conflict between the theory theory and the simulation view. Simulation can occur only when one has a mental concept that can be applied equally to self and other. This follows from the earlier argument that subjective experience is *not* introspectable without concepts. Theory theory, on the other hand, correctly captures the importance of linguistic concepts in cognitive development. The central problem, that neither view adequately captures, is that concepts may be identified with the *sense* of a word or expression. I defended the view that the concept comes into existence with the acquisition of a word or expression. I return to the relationship between the feeling that something makes sense and concept of understanding in Chapter 11.

JACKENDOFF'S THEORY OF MEANING

Ray Jackendoff (2012) is a Chomskian linguist who takes cognition seriously (just as I am a cognitivist who takes linguistics seriously). He takes as fundamental the question of how perception and perceptual knowledge are related to linguistic expressions. Like Gopnik and Meltzoff, Jackendoff wants to "pull meanings and concepts together and say that the meaning of a word is the concept it expresses" (pp. 70–71), adding that a word is little more than a concept with a phonological tag. I agree. However, Jackendoff implies that the concept preexists the language although he recognizes the dilemma of both saying that preverbal children have concepts and at the same time saying that concepts are word meanings. To avoid a quibble over the use of the term "concept," he mischievously offers the notion of "goncepts," which are concept-like cognitions that become linguistic concepts when they acquire a phonology. I question the existence of nonlinguistic concepts offering in their place an enriched notion of subjective feelings. Instead of a pre-linguistic language of thought, I would suggest that concepts and the language of thought come into existence with the acquisition of language. Learning a word is learning a phonological symbol with a *sense* as distinct from its reference as Frege demonstrated. Thus, for me, the direction of explanation is reversed: words create concepts rather than merely express them.

REPRESENTATIONAL THEORY OF MIND

Jerry Fodor (1975; see also "Mental representation" *Stanford Encyclopedia of Philosophy*) is often credited with the modern philosophical or psychological Representational Theory of Mind (RTM), a framework that essentially defines cognitive science. RTM explains observable behavior by attributing codes, concepts, rules, mental maps to intelligent systems, including those of human adults, infants, other animals, and computers. These mental representations are said to exist independently of language and, indeed, to make the learning of language possible. Fodor takes the RTM further, seeing these codes and concepts as an innate language of thought (LOT). Mental concepts such as "believe" and "understand" are said to be already available innately to be called up as processing resources develop. In my view, the LOT theory falls afoul of Wittgenstein's arguments against a private language. Wittgenstein argued that a language is necessarily public, shared with, and corrected by others to meet an agreed standard. The public language argument casts doubt on a private LOT. Recall that the concept of "understand" included in its identity criteria not only correctness but also intersubjectivity. Of course, once a public language is acquired, it may function as RTM. RTM, then, is a linguistic mind; that is, the theory of mind is composed on lexical concepts composed of a phonology (or visual sign), a place in the grammar (a noun), with a *sense* as distinguished from its reference. (Fodor dismisses the private language argument.)[1] This shared inter-subjectivity is what makes language applicable to a shared objective reality as true or false and applicable to self and others. Words are acquired in part because they may be used to refer to things including the pre-conceptual affective states. Words have a *sense* composed of identity criteria that classify and distinguish states from one another.

In rejecting Fodor's nativism, I also cast doubt on the entire notion of mental representation and RTM. This is in spite of the fact that I have spent most of my academic life attempting to characterize early cognitions in terms of mental representations or, as I framed it, how young subjects "code" the stimulus situations they encountered. In this, I was a follower of Bruner's "new look," the claim that stimuli were never simply given but taken up in the light of prior knowledge. As assumed by RTM, children's knowledge was described in terms of mental representations, cognitive maps, categories, concepts, beliefs, and strategies. Since beliefs and other representations were seen as the basic furniture of cognition, the concept of belief was treated as metarepresentational, that is, a belief about a belief (Perner, 1991). I would claim, rather, that pre-linguistic cognitions are not beliefs but feelings; beliefs appear only with linguistic concepts, thereby collaps-ing the difference between a belief and a concept of belief. There are no beliefs without the concept of belief as Davidson has argued. Belief, like understanding, is a verbal concept, essentially a word with a sense and a reference, with a role in a sentence that is true or false. What I had overlooked earlier was the possibility that the mental codes young children formulated were limited by the linguistic concepts they had acquired.

---

[1] When, at a meeting in Toronto in 1989, Gopnik, Astington, and I told Fodor that children were no more able to ascribe beliefs to themselves than they were to others, Fodor stared at us with disbelief. He insisted that believing was innate. It was just what minds do. I still regard Fodor as the leading genius of the field.

I have sketched out an alternative to RTM in terms of cognitive–affective processes that are responsive to situations in the light of prior similar experience that regulate action and that monitor outcomes in terms of feeling tone. Although highly adaptive, feelings are nonlogical, non-categorical, and nonconceptual. They are beautifully innocent in that they are experienced but, prior to the appropriate language, unavailable to introspection or to thought. The linguistic system, in contrast, is representational, categorical, and conceptual and of which the RTM is a largely correct description. There is a language of thought, as Fodor insisted, but that language is not an innate language but a natural language such as English or Swahili (Olson & Campbell, 1993). I have sketched out two systems, the feeling system and conceptual system and the relationship between them in terms of similarity and differences of their identity conditions. For concepts, I identified these identity conditions with the Fregean *senses* of words and expressions.

COMPREHENSION THEORY

Comprehension theory as set out by Kintsch (1998) was described earlier. Here I consider the relation of that theory to the one I have outlined.

The goal of reading a text is understanding it. This is achieved, as Kintsch showed, by satisfying two constraints: the beliefs and goals of the reader, and the linguistic structure of expression or text. His computational model offers a plausible account of how this is achieved. I have not attempted to say precisely how this is achieved, suggesting rather that understanding is knowing the conditions to be met in judging that one understands. These constraints were the identity criteria for understanding, correctness, and intersubjectivity. The Kintsch model is an account that honors but leaves implicit these criteria, correctness is the standard set by the expert, and mutuality is assumed to be at least reachable through teaching and argument. Experts show readers where they went wrong. Ascription of understanding is made by the teacher. In my view, three factors are overlooked. There is no account of how the reader ascribes or judges his or her own understanding, and there is no account of what it feels like to understand. Third, although the comprehension model highlights both prior knowledge and linguistic form, it lacks a clear account of how that prior knowledge directs the linguistic processing. In my view, comprehension is, as ML has demonstrated, prediction or anticipation of what may be plausibly said. The reader's beliefs and goals are foregrounded; reading is the attempt by the reader to detect linguistic information that bears on the truth and validity of those preexisting beliefs. Counter to Kintsch's model, there is no stage of first reading the sentence and then understanding it.

Comprehension monitoring is a matter of bringing these criteria under scrutiny, requiring the listener or reader to attend to the properties of text or context that justify the claim that understanding has in fact been achieved. Comprehension monitoring calls for the giving of reasons that justify the criteria of correctness and intersubjectivity.

LINGUISTIC DETERMINISM

Linguistic determinism is the claim that what we can think is both limited by and enabled by what we can say. Some psycholinguists have defended the view that cognitive development is, in fact, linguistic development. Gleitman (1990), for example, argued that mental verbs are acquired through a kind of "syntactic bootstrapping," using the syntax as a clue to the meaning of mental verbs. Karmiloff-Smith (1992) showed that learning about "more than one" was accompanied by learning the plural marker /s/. Pinker (1994) extended this view by proposing that "semantic bootstrapping" involved mapping a cognitive system to a grammatical system.

deVilliers (2005, p. 200), a self-declared linguistic determinist, derived her determinism not from Whorf but from Chomsky's generative grammar. The idea is that the semantic structures of language, words and grammar, both limit and enable forms of thought. deVilliers's specific contribution is to show how grammatical development, the ability to formulate more complex complement clauses, enables children to understand false belief and to ascribe beliefs to themselves and others. Young children do not entertain false beliefs; they reject them as Roy Pea's subject did in denying that a peach was an orange. DeVilliers showed that the false belief task requires some way to treat an expression, not by rejecting it as false but by incorporating it into a true belief by the grammatical device of a complement clause. "I believe that the candy is in the box but Maxi thinks *that* it is in the drawer." On its own, "the candy is in the drawer" is false, but by means of the pronoun "that," the speaker allows that it may be believed by Maxi. The thought is enabled by the acquisition of a particular grammatical device, the complement clause.

Verbs as well as nouns enable thoughts. deVilliers examined children's acquisition of the verb "want." Children use the word not only to make requests but also soon begin to use the word in more complex grammatical forms such as "He wants a car; He wants to buy a car; He wants Jane to buy a car." In this way, the meaning of the word parts course, at least to some extent, with the subjective feeling of desire. Consequently, the word allows not only the expression of desire but also the *ascription* of desire to oneself and others in both the present and the past tense. Ascriptions, being verbal, are necessarily categorical and propositional, dependent on the possession of a grammar. Once it is granted that language is generative, it becomes clear that language is not only a constraint on thought but also the very power of thought. Language gives us the power to think anything at all within the range of the sayable.

deVilliers concluded that the concept of thinking is a consequence of acquiring the grammar. She claimed that the child could not entertain a false belief without the linguistic competence needed for expressing the concept. I treat this claim as identical to my claim that the concept of understanding does not exist without words but rather comes into being with learning the word "understanding" with its distinct *sense* and its place in the grammar.

Of course, this is not to say that preverbal children and other animals lack desires but rather to say that language turns desires and feelings into concepts formed through learning words.

RATIONAL EMOTIONS

The distinction I have drawn between feeling and linguistic concepts for representing those feelings derives some support from Joseph Heath's (2011) defense of the rationality of emotions. He argued that the acquisition of a language turns feelings into linguistic concepts, objects of thought to which rational rules may be applied. Acquiring concepts like good and bad not only expresses feelings but also propositionalizes them, turning them into objects of thought to which the rules of logic apply. As the concepts become more elaborated, the feelings become more refined, as I have described in Chapter 3.

TWO SYSTEMS THEORY

The Two Systems Theory of Mind offers a general theory that, in part, captures the distinction between subjective feelings and objective concepts. Keith Stanovich (1999) in his study of reasoning tasks found that he could divide patterns of responses into two basic categories that he called System 1 and System 2. Responses classed as System 1 tended to be fast, habitual, intuitive, and holistic. Those classed as System 2 tended to be slow, rational, and logical. Stanovich traces his distinction to the work of Sloman (1996) who distinguished an associative processing system that responds primarily on the basis of similarity and contiguity from a rule-based system that operates on logically organized symbolic systems. Although Stanovich applied the Two System theory only to linguistic reasoning tasks, he suggested that the approach may be applicable to young children and other nonhuman species. Stanovich claimed that System 2 captured something analogous to taking a second look.

Kahneman (2011) generated considerable interest in the two systems in his account of two ways of thinking, one fast and the other slow. Slow thinking depended on careful linguistic analysis, the precise meaning of terms such as "probable," and judgments of relevance of information to any decision. In fact, Kahneman's tasks are similar to those used in the Comprehension Monitoring experiments, to be

Table 10.1. *Two Systems theory*

Stanovich's Two Systems		Olson's Two Systems	
SYSTEM 1	SYSTEM 2	FEELINGS	CONCEPTS
Associative	Rule-based	Affective	Rational
Holistic	Analytic	Perceptual	Linguistic
Automatic	Controlled	Analogue	Digital
Undemanding	Demanding	Valorized	Neutralized
Relatively fast	Relatively slow	Procedural	Propositional
Habitual	Cultural	Good-Bad	True-False
Contextualized	Decontextualized	Egocentric	Sociocentric
Personalized	Depersonalized	Commitments	Beliefs
Biases?	Heuristics?	Sentient	Sapient

discussed more fully in Chapter 11. Stanovich took the additional step of associating correct interpretation as a sign of rationality. For my purposes, it is the categories themselves that may elucidate the relationship between feeling states and cognitive ones. The distinctive properties of Stanovich's Two Systems is shown on the left half of Table 10.1. On the right half of Table 10.1 are listed the features that distinguish subjective feelings from linguistic concepts that I drew from the work of Proust, Nussbaum, Taylor and Jackendoff (2012). The former describes a form of consciousness that Brandom (1994) called "sentient," an awareness of what is happening and what an organism should do about it. The second is the conceptual, linguistic system that Brandom called "sapient" (attuned to reason).

It is clear that the classifications serve different purposes. All of Stanovich's and Kahneman's tasks are verbal and attribute differences to heuristic strategies and biases such as a confirmation bias. There is no simple match between heuristics and biases on one hand and System 1 and System 2 on the other. It remains to be seen if "biases" can be analyzed in terms of the truth preserving assumption discussed in Chapter 4, where I argued that understanding is always in the service of the fixation and updating of belief.

The affective–conceptual contrast on the right side of the table assumes a real difference in the cognitive functions of creatures with language and those without language, whether in animals, young children, or computers. The concern here is with the uniqueness of the systems and the relationship between them.

Dual Process theory captures the important difference between nonlinguistic competencies and linguistic, rational ones but offers little to an explanation of how feelings are related to conceptual states or to an explanation of mental states or how such states are ascribed. On the positive side, the heuristics and biases proposals highlights a basic fact about understanding language, namely the overwhelming significance of "bias," the beliefs and expectancies of the listener or reader, of what I earlier called "taking as true" that listeners and readers bring to the interpretation of any expression. The best any sentence can do is tune up these expectancies. I return to this issue in my discussion of rhetorical speech in Chapter 13.

PHILOSOPHY AND EDUCATION

Bakhurst (2011) examined the relevance of analytical philosophy to developmental psychology and to the role of education in the formation of a rational mind. Building on the work of Sellars, McDowell, Wittgenstein, and Davidson, Bakhurst argued that children acquire a "second nature" as they learn the language of the culture. He described children's cognitive development as a series of stage-like achievements built around learning a language. To learn the language is to acquire a "second nature." Learning the type–token relation reflects the acquisition of definite and indefinite articles, the acquisition of concepts reflects the acquisition of the word meanings, and reflective thinking reflects learning to meet standards of correctness by appeal to reasons and evidence. Through language, children enter what Sellars (1997) had called "the space of reasons." Although Bakhurst drew heavily on Vygotsky and "his Russians," he is very critical of such social notions as social construction, internalization, and appropriation of culture that tend to undermine the importance of the individual, self-conscious, responsible self.

However, in my view, Bakhurst overestimated the pre-linguistic cognitions that I have called feelings. He overestimated by claiming, "There is no question that the pre-linguistic child can 'think and act intentionally' in a perfectly uncontentious sense of those terms" (p. 9). In my view, the ascription of thoughts and intentions should be restricted to those creatures with knowledge of a public language. Second, like Janack, Bakhurst defended the primacy of first-person subjective experience. I argued, on the other hand, that subjective states may be experienced but become objects of thought only through language. Introspection is self-ascription, and self-ascription is based on the same identity conditions as other-ascription. Concepts, as linguistic *senses*, are public and equally applicable to self and other. Nonetheless, I see Bakhurst's work on "second nature" as basic to an account of mind and the role of the school in its development. More empirical evidence for these theoretical claims is required.

LANGUAGE AS EXPLICITNESS

Brandom's (1994) distinction between "sentience" and "sapience" captures the distinction I make between feelings and concepts. Sentience, as mentioned earlier, is the consciousness available to nonhuman animals and to young children; "sapience," on the other hand, is the consciousness connected to concepts and reason. Reason is essentially a linguistic process, a matter of finding words to make statements and hold beliefs. Brandom called the move from sentience to sapience a matter of "making explicit," that is, formulating prior behavioral and social practices into a linguistic, propositional form. Making explicit involves, as Sellars and Bakhurst argued, inventing or learning a verbal concept. Like Brandom, I identified the concept with a word meaning (or its paraphrase), and while the word comes from hearing the language, the reference for the word such as "sad" comes from the nonconceptual content of the feelings.

Have Sellars, Brandom, and Bakhurst gone beyond Dewey who is still the dominant figure in educational theory? Yes, in that Dewey had an outdated theory of language. Dewey is famous for his attack on "book learning" and his claim that one could learn by doing. By linking knowledge to success in practical action, Dewey conflated success and understanding. Understanding, like knowledge, involves a normative standard of correctness and truth; only language allows one to formulate belief-like propositions that may be evaluated for their truth by others. In other words, Dewey would not be credited with having made what Rorty (1981) called "the linguistic turn." An improvement on Dewey would involve an acknowledgment of the unique position of language in the formation of the concepts in general and of the concepts of belief and understanding, in particular, a step taken by Brandom.

Brandom not only identifies concepts with word meaning but also sides with Chomskian linguistics. Language is not merely a set of linguistic concepts expressive of one's beliefs; they enable the formation of beliefs. For Chomsky, language is a generative syntactic system that potentially links every concept with every other concept. Young children learning a language suddenly discover this generative power as any observation of a three-year-old will demonstrate and as documented by Ruth Weir's (1962) recordings of a young child's bedtime monologues. The torrent of the speech of many three-year-olds is daunting. Yet many years of experience and schooling may be necessary for children to work out the relationship amongst the concepts they acquire. Children learn concepts such as "up" and "down" contrastively, yet, I have observed, it is not until the early school years that they recognize that "up" is the opposite of "down" or that, as we saw earlier, "more" can be replaced by "less" if the situation calls for it, as we saw in Figure 5.1.

VYGOTSKY

Vygotsky (1986) took a decisive step in the direction I am defending when he identified the word as the fundamental unit of mind. It is also a fair question for developmental psychologists to ask if Brandom's claim that a concept is simply a word meaning is an advance over Vygotsky's (1986, p. 256) claim that "[a] word is a microcosm of human consciousness." There is some controversy as to whether Vygotsky grasped the sense–reference distinction. Both Fodor (1972) and Wertsch (2000) have argued that he did not. Vygotsky (1986, pp. 222–224) had claimed that when children were asked about a word, they pointed to the reference object. He wrote, "[T]he word to the child is an integral part of the object" and again that "the meaning of a word is a complex of concrete objects connected by a factual tie," both of which suggest a conflation of sense and reference. Vygotsky advanced the notion of "scientific concepts," those acquired in school, to explain how and when terms came to be defined in terms of each other. Derry (2013) argued that indeed Vygotsky conceived of meaning in a more complex way as embodying a "system of judgments" and rejected Wertsch's notion of "decontextualization" as a possible explanation of meaning. Certainly Vygotsky's followers such as Liublinskaya (1957) not only made the sense–reference distinction but also provided evidence that even children's first words applied not only to the objects used as exemplars in training but also to novel objects. Thus, children who learned the word "red" in a discrimination task not only applied it to novel objects but also, having learned to distinguish objects on the basis of "red," more easily learned to discriminate objects on the basis of another color, yellow. Thus, the *sense* of the word "red" includes that red is a color; discriminating red objects does not.

It seems clear that even young children in learning a word acquire a *sense* that carried over across different referent objects but that they have limited knowledge of the mappings amongst words. As Vygotsky pointed out, these relations come to the fore in systematic teaching. The ability to provide formal definitions, as Vygotsky argued, is a scholarly enterprise. Yet even ordinary concepts such as "white" or "round" are not islands but linked to others. You cannot know "white" without knowing that the word applies to a range of objects and that "white" is a color, as children demonstrate when they answer "What color is that?" or when they transfer what they learned about "red" to learning "yellow." Some further evidence for this claim comes from the discrimination learning experiments of Kendler and Kendler (1959). They showed that kindergarten children who easily learned to choose white over black also readily learned to switch their response, to choose black over white, a so-called reversal shift. I see this as a kind of nonverbal opposites task that shows that in learning the concept of white, one is also learning that white is a color. As Macnamara (1986) pointed out, one cannot know a thing unless it is seen as a kind of a thing. The kind is what is captured by the *sense* of a word.

In my view, Vygotsky's and Brandom's claims are roughly equivalent. However, as educational philosophers Derry (2013) and Bakhurst (2011) have both pointed out, the followers of Vygotsky have become so wedded to personal meaning and sense-making that they have lost sight of standards for the correctness of understanding and the objectivity of knowledge. By insisting, with Brandom, that the senses of words have an objective value that permit the formation of statements that may be judged as true or false, the analytic tradition brings a new objectivity to our science of mind and a new standard for the goals of education.

All these lines of evidence support my first claim, namely that concepts, the units of thought, are word meanings and, consequently, that the concept of understanding can be reduced to the meaning or *sense* of the word "understand." However, that research says nothing about the second of my central claims, namely that the act of ascription of understanding itself is what makes understanding rational. The act of ascription matters because it is the act of ascribing understanding, as opposed to having understanding ascribed to one, that requires one to justify their understanding by appeal to reason and evidence. This was the subject of Chapter 8, and I return to it in Chapter 11.

11 Understanding and Sense-Making

Understanding is both the means and goal of learning through language. I contrast two traditions that appear in psychological and educational thought that draw on the concepts of meaning and understanding. One emphasizes the importance of subjective mental states and treats meaning as personal significance, that is, something that "makes sense" to the reader. The other emphasizes the importance of correct understanding and treats meaning as an objective achievement that meets the criteria specified by the sense of the word "understand," namely correctness and intersubjectivity.

Making sense is the subjective experience that allows the child or other animal the confidence to go on, to expect that the world is unfolding much as it has in the past. Such subjective states are manifest to us as observers as interest, curiosity, and a willingness to go on, to learn and even to repeat an activity and enjoy the satisfactions of achieving one's goals. We adults know such feelings and we attribute them to the children.

Subjective feelings are necessary but not sufficient for the ascription of understanding. The subjective feeling of understanding may or may not meet the conditions for an objectively correct understanding. The first, I said, is the feeling that something makes sense, allowing one to go on, and the second is the concept of understanding with its conditions of truth and intersubjectivity. Clearly, these are not equivalent. A child or a student may think he or she understands, while the teacher insists that he or she does not. The child's willingness to continue may be based on the feeling of understanding, the teacher's, on meeting objective criteria.

Making sense is the response of a listener or reader to an expression; it is the personal meaning or significance to them of an expression or text. These subjective feelings, long ignored in philosophy and psychology, have been revived by writers such as Janack (2012), who, as I pointed out earlier, took her lead from Bruner (1990) and who accused cognitive science "of dehumanizing the very concept of mind." The originating impulse of the cognitive revolution, Bruner wrote, was the "conviction that the central concept of a human psychology is *meaning* and the processes and transactions involved in the construction of meanings" (1990, p. 33). The meanings of greatest interest to Bruner were those of deeply held personal significance that are embedded in practical action and in the cultural practices such as those involved in narrative (Amsterdam, 2000). Stories are important, he argued, in that they are the means by which we make sense of our lives and the world around us. The proper topic of psychology, he claimed, is what makes sense to us, the meanings and commitments that we live by. Hence, for Bruner, meaning is not the correct meaning assigned to a text but rather the personal beliefs and commitments of the reader that result from the personal understanding of an expression. Indeed, Bruner dismisses analytical philosophers and computationalists as being concerned only with correctness while excluding the deep feelings of understanding he called meaning. In this, Bruner is at one with Dewey and the Progressives, who insisted that what is learned from experience is not or not only justifiably objective truth but what makes sense to the learner.

    In identifying meaning with personal significance, Bruner runs afoul of Frege's rejection of this commonsense meaning of meaning. Frege, recall, claimed that meaning should be replaced by the sense-reference distinction. The *sense* of a word, Frege claimed, was objective, definable, and suitable for systematic thought, whereas the subjective notion of meaning remained unmoored. Bruner did refer to Frege's distinction between *sense* and reference, reference bearing on truth and *sense* as established by the relations "to other sentences" (p. 62). However, he then dismissed this notion of sense, as it is "independent of any particular or private sense" (p. 62). Bruner wanted to capture private sense, first-person subjectivity, that is, what has significance for the person. He added, "Under this [Fregean] dispensation, meaning became a philosopher's tool, a formal instrument of logical analysis." What Bruner wanted to add was personal meaning, the beliefs and commitments one is prepared to live by and that can be refined by reading and other forms of experience. But in so doing, he forfeited the objectivity of understanding, the understanding that meets both of our criteria, correctness and intersubjectivity.

It could be argued that Bruner "solved" the objectivity problem by arguing that meaning is always social and learned through the social interactions of speakers who monitor and correct each other's understandings. If so, his espousal of personal meaning is not deeply at odds with impersonal, objective meaning; rather, it is a matter of emphasis. Whatever his intention, followers of Bruner like those of Vygotsky often take the achievement of subjective meaning – that is, of sense-making – as an appropriate goal of understanding. In so doing, they may underestimate the importance of correctness, that is, the objectively correct meaning warranted and justified by evidence and reason.

Subjective feelings are drawn from one's deepest beliefs, values, personal commitments, and feelings of security. These are the "priors" that listeners bring to any expression. They provide the context in terms of which any expression makes sense. This feeling is nonconceptual and may occur even if, by objective standards such as passing a test, correct understanding was not achieved. These feelings are ongoing and continuous. Teachers recognize these feelings not only in fidgeting when making sense lapses but also in facial expressions of interest, engagement, and boredom. To date, objective measures of these feeling in relation to reading and understanding are lacking but may become available as the study of other emotions, especially the emotions involved in learning, progresses. I see this as a field for important future research on understanding.

Bruner's emphasis on meaning, meaning-making, and sense-making both is widely adopted in psychology and education and, while important, as we have seen, is somewhat misleading. His emphasis on subjective meanings has left him open to the charge that he has ignored the objective standards for correct understanding, the standard set by the school and society, and justified by evidence and reason. In so doing, his critics say, he undermined the concern with truth and correctness, that is, meeting objective standards.

Indeed, teachers are faced with a dilemma in educating children. Their dilemma is just that articulated by Bruner. They are torn between meeting a fixed standard and encouraging the mental activities, the sense-making of children. Teachers themselves tend to take the feelings of children as an indication of and a suitable outcome for teaching. Authorities rely more on objective assessments, meeting the objective standards known to the expert, those embodied in the textbook, and the teacher. That teachers must respect and honor the learner's feelings of understanding or not understanding seems to me beyond question. But feelings are not enough.

Bruner's emphasis on personal meaning and significance has been completely overshadowed by the successes of computationalism in psychology and objective testing in education. In cognitive science, passing the Turing test is accepted as evidence of understanding. In studies of comprehension and comprehension monitoring, correctness is the only criterion that is monitored. Similarly, in school, passing an objective test is taken as an objective criterion for understanding. So successful is computationalism in explaining some aspects of intelligence and understanding that it threatens to redefine those concepts in computational terms while attracting much of the research and research funding to that project. Subjectivity, of the sort Bruner and Janack (and now I) champion, is either denied completely or relegated to soft sciences of education and health care. While subjective experience is important, there is more to understanding than just personal commitment; there is truth. It is the computationalists' focus on truth that has eclipsed Bruner's and Janack's attention to subjective sense-making.

In sum, young children understanding may be limited to what "makes sense" to them rather than the understanding implied by the possession of an ascribable concept. Although the feeling of understanding falls short of correct understanding, its significance is not to be underestimated. Little is known about the feelings evoked in young children when they understand or when they fail to understand. "Look-backs" are evidence that comprehension faltered, that something does not make sense, but there are few visible signs when comprehension proceeds smoothly.

As mentioned earlier, this is a topic ripe for research. Feelings of interest, relevance, progress, plausibility, and certainty ("Are you sure?") are arguably as important to understanding as the ability to justify one's understanding by appeal to the relevant evidence.

Furthermore, all listeners and readers, including adults, rely primarily upon the subjective criterion of making sense, that is, on the subjective "feeling of understanding" that maintains their interest and advances their beliefs. Adults' commitments to what "makes sense" to them often completely overwhelms any contradictory evidence presented to them. I discuss this further in the case of political rhetoric in Chapter 13.

The subjective feeling of understanding provides both motivation for and enjoyment of reading. Consequently, modern textbooks for the "language arts" in Ontario, Canada, place more emphasis on sense-making, what engages individual learners and keeps them reading, than on correctness (Tomkins, Bright & Winsor, 2018). Sense-making, what the reader makes of experience, is of a piece with discovery learning and learning by doing – educational practices advocated by Dewey, Piaget, and Bruner. Clearly, this position is not only at odds with government accountability policy that stresses meeting objective standards but also falls short of the very notion of what we mean by "understanding."

In a recent analysis of reading and reading pedagogy, Seidenberg (2017, p. 261ff.) attributed the decline in reading scores to the child-centered pedagogies that have equated what makes sense to a reader with objectively correct understanding. He claimed child-centered pedagogies have embraced an "educational worldview [that] takes subjectivity as an existential condition." What "makes sense" to a reader, even that achieved through guessing, he argued, is given equal weight to correctness of a reading. Correctness, of course, depends largely on honoring the lexical, syntactic, and pragmatic properties of the expressions. Seidenberg found inexplicable that educators could pit a concern with meaning against a concern with linguistic structure, understanding versus phonemic awareness, for example, in designing educational programs. I second his alarm and concern.

But while correctly pointing out the problems created by emphasizing subjective sense-making at the expense of objective correctness, Seidenberg then created a similar problem by emphasizing the importance of meeting objective criteria while disregarding entirely the concern of most educators, namely the educational experience itself, the interest and engagement, and subjective understandings and beliefs of the learners themselves. He showed complete disregard for what learners bring to their encounters with print; what they think they are doing, trying to do, want to do; and the feelings of success and failure that allow learners to go on. These feeling are presumably involved in every educational transaction. Thus, rather than resolving the harmful polarities that tend to dominate educational theory and practice, Seidenberg raised them anew in his home state, Wisconsin, where, like the United States more generally, public education and the teaching profession are under threat, and privatizing education is well under way, encouraged by former president Trump's then education secretary, Betsy DeVos. Seidenberg did give voice to his most serious critic and advocate for public schooling, Diane Ravitch (2011, 2021).

In Seidenberg's analysis of reading for understanding, there are no agents, no beliefs, no intentions, no anticipations, no expectancies, no interest, no sense-making, no feelings, no learner's point of view.

Perhaps these important features have been simply taken for granted so that he could focus on measurable skills and outcomes. Perhaps, like the Behaviorists, he denies subjective experience altogether. Consequently, his focus on measureable achievable outcomes is paid for by his complete dismissal of the learner's point of view and, with it, the appropriateness of a teacher's attention to what children think. It would be an error to compound Seidenberg denunciation of subjectivity by a corresponding denunciation of objective knowledge and objective standards. It is the way they are linked that is important. It is worth noting that Seidenberg's interpretation of the cognitive revolution is precisely what alarmed Bruner and has now alarmed Janack, namely the eclipse of subjective experience. Seidenberg did highlight the importance of objective standards, that those of us, long sympathetic to Vygotsky and Bruner, have not always faced up to.

It is important to not let the discourse about teaching reading and teaching understanding degenerate, yet again, into polemics. Seidenberg made a valid claim that educational theory and practice often take interest and engagement as suitable alternatives to the assessment of actual correct behavior. Subjectivity is not a sufficient condition for acquiring knowledge but is a necessary condition in that it is the learner who does the learning. All learning, in my view, has to meet the standard of making sense to the learner. Otherwise, it is memorization, not understanding.

The more appropriate question is how one encourages engagement and subjective experience of readers, goals that have been stressed by generations of teachers and librarians, while at the same time encouraging the mastery of objective accessible skills such as word recognition, phoneme–grapheme relations, and spelling and answering comprehension questions. Engagement is as much the product of correct understanding as it is a precondition for it. These are not alternatives. The ability to ascribe understanding provides a common ground between child and teacher in that the identity conditions for understanding include both correctness and intersubjectivity. Ascribing understanding calls for judgment as to the conditions to be met and the evidence relevant to the ascription. Ascription, as I argued in Chapter 8, is what turns understanding into a rational process dependent on the giving of reasons. The provision of reasons is the route to intersubjectivity, to reaching an agreement between learner and teacher. Readers often fail to achieve this standard, and I return to this question in Chapter 12.

So we come full circle. The learner or reader may have a feeling of understanding but that is no guarantee that he or she has actually achieved understanding. On the other hand, understanding may be ascribed "to" the child if its behavior meets the criteria for understanding even if the child lacks the ability to ascribe understanding. When children learn to ascribe understanding to themselves and others, they encounter the need for evidence and reasons justifying their ascriptions. Ascribing understanding, so to speak, is giving one's word that understanding has been achieved. When achieved, the learner knows they understand and feels secure in their knowledge. They both understand and feel that they understand.

Mental concepts not only are for ascribing to others but also are the tools for self-ascription, reflection, and introspection for learners themselves. Consider the case of my five-year-old granddaughter, Hannah. "Who lives there?" she asked as we passed a derelict house down the street. "I don't know," I answered. This followed one of those long delays that betrays deep thought. Finally she replied, "I don't know either." Clearly she had the feeling that she did not know who lived in that house, a feeling that provoked her question "Who lives there?" When I replied that I didn't know, she was perplexed. But what provoked her comment "I don't know either"? Apparently, she hadn't *known* that she didn't know; she just didn't know. The word now provided a tool for thinking about her own mental state. An opening to a life of the mind – this is the subject of the next chapter, Chapter 12.

12 Understanding As a Learnable Skill

Student understanding of what they read is a primary concern of the school, but student achievement of this goal is often judged as unsatisfactory. Extensive psychological and educational research has been directed to improving student understanding and explaining student failure. Understanding in this context is treated as a trainable skill. The alternative is to treat understanding as learning to meet the conditions for correct ascription of understanding to self and others.

In this chapter, I pick up the theme advanced in Chapter 8 where I distinguished between ascription of understanding *to* subjects whether by parent, teacher, or scientist, to the ascription of understanding *by* subjects themselves. We adults ascribe understanding to children when we judge that their behavior meets the criteria for understanding, namely correctness and intersubjectivity. It is we as ascribers who make the judgment. Here I focus on the second part, namely how the children ascribe understanding whether to themselves or to others. That is, I consider the benefits that accrue to the children when they themselves learn to make ascriptions of understanding. I have already hinted at the answer: To ascribe is to judge that an interpretation has met the standards of correctness and intersubjectivity and to justify the ascription by appeal to the evidence that can warrant the judgment.

ASCRIBED "TO"

We ascribe understanding to systems, whether young child, other animal, or computer or even adults when their behavior meets the identity criteria, correctness and intersubjectivity. So long as their responses meet the adult standard, we attribute understanding to them; children pass the test, and computers make correct responses. Just how they met those standards are irrelevant so long as they are met.

As we saw in Chapter 2, what computers are doing in order to meet our criteria is essentially unknown to us. As Baecker (2019) pointed out, ML is highly successful, but because responses are determined by the system as a whole, it is impossible to know what the system knows or does not know. The mental states and processes of young children and other animals are only slightly less mysterious. How they meet these criteria may be irrelevant in any case. When they give a correct answer, we ascribe understanding because their performance meets the identity criteria set by the meaning of the word and concept of "understand." When young children are asked "Where does Maxi think the candy is?" and they mistakenly report where the candy actually is, they are not simply wrong. They have given an answer that "makes sense" to them, that they cheerfully and confidently affirm. Sense-making, I have argued, is the understanding that permits the child to "go on." What allows one to "go on" is that the expression is believable and plausible even if the objective criteria for understanding have not been met. Sense-making, as I argued in Chapter 11, is the feeling of understanding, an emotion based on an appraisal of the situation in terms of prior experience, expectancies as to what is likely to happen and what to do about it as well as a phenomenal feeling tone. Importantly, the feeling of understanding does not meet the standard of correctness for understanding.

ASCRIPTION "BY"

Understanding, unlike the feeling of understanding, has truth or correctness as part of its meaning. To understand is to understand correctly. It is on the basis of evidence that these criteria have been met that adults ascribe understanding to children and computers. We say that a child understands because *we* appraise their behavior in the light of these criteria: correctness and intersubjectivity. But here is the critical point: what happens when it is the learner himself or herself, who does the ascribing, and who makes the judgment? Here the ascription is "by" the learner, not only "to" the learner. In order to ascribe understanding correctly, one must know that the conditions for understanding include truth and intersubjectivity and know that these conditions have been met. This is the straightforward consequence of the fact that ascribing understanding is making a claim that understanding has occurred. It is a claim that is true or false and for which the ascriber is responsible and accountable. Ascribing is what J. L. Austin (1962) called a speech act, the act of asserting something as true, of giving one's word that such and such is the case. One can make such an assertion only if one has reasons that would justify the claim. Giving reasons is what makes ascription a rational action. When we ascribe understanding *to* children and computers, we do so for our reasons, but we make no claim that the objects or persons we ascribe understanding to know or share those reasons. Children's learning to ascribe understanding, then, is not only a worthy educational goal but also a topic worthy of research.

My proposal is that language comprehension may be seen as demanding what I called "ascribing by" rather than "ascribing to." It is the act of ascription that brings into prominence the criteria to be used in judging or ascribing understanding to oneself or others. To ascribe understanding is to judge that understanding has been achieved, a judgment that may be justified by appeal to evidence for correctness and intersubjectivity.

In order to ascribe understanding ("ascribe by"), one must know or judge that the required criteria – correctness and intersubjectivity – have been met. Correctness would be decided on much the same basis as any scientific or legal judgment, namely that it be justifiable by reason and available evidence. In the final analysis, institutions such as the Academy (as did the French Academy in the seventeenth century) or the sciences, the courts, the church, or the school monitor and attempt to uphold the standard for correctness by defining terms, setting out rules for correct grammar, for written prose, and so on. These rules are tested even in everyday discourse when someone

challenges a speaker by asking "What do you mean?" expecting clarification. Ascription is not merely description; it is an assertion or
claim for which one is responsible and accountable, as I argued in
Chapter 8.

Ascribing understanding and justifying the ascription by appeal
to reason and evidence is required in all forms of reasoning but is not
easily achieved. Peter Carruthers (2007, p. 206) argued that most
people

> are bad at reasoning about reasoning—at identifying mistakes in
> reasoning, at theorizing about standards of good reasoning, and at
> improving their own and others' reasoning. Yet this is precisely the
> competence that the self-monitoring model predicts we
> should have.

> Bodies of beliefs [about beliefs] have to be laboriously acquired
> through processes of formal education. They include the canons of
> good scientific method, developed piecemeal over the last five
> centuries or so, as well as principles of validity, codified in systems
> of logic. This isn't a natural competence but a deliberately socially
> transmitted one.

Teachers report that children have difficulty with providing reasons
for their answers and there is some evidence that less-educated adults
treat requests for clarification of meaning as threatening and
"requests for reasons as 'agonistic'" (Malinowski, 1923, p. 451).

Recent research directed at the improving reading comprehension
focus on what is called comprehension monitoring. Comprehension
monitoring was introduced as a form of metacognition by John Flavell
(1981; see the papers in Dickson, 1981) and his colleagues (Markman,
1981). This research has demonstrated that even high school graduates
wildly overestimate their ability to remember and understand what
they read. Researchers traced this failure to the possibility that students
failed to monitor their comprehension. Monitoring comprehension
would involve not simply giving the correct answer but also to "trying

to summarize, paraphrase, find examples of, make inferences from, expand on, ask questions about, or put into practice," practices that student could use to assure themselves that they had correctly understood (pp. 53–54). This provided a basis for a productive research program with important educational implications.

Studies by Brown (1975), Bereiter and Scardamalia (1993), and others have shown that children's comprehension can be markedly improved if they are shown that their own criteria for understanding are inadequate or inappropriate for certain tasks and that comprehension improved markedly if they are taught strategies for monitoring their understanding.

Adults ascribe understanding to students if the correct answer is given, whether the students can justify their answer or not. On the other hand, when the child or student himself or herself ascribes understanding (ascribe by), they can do so only if they know the conditions for correct ascription and consider the evidence and reasons that would justify the ascription.

Whereas comprehension monitoring assumes that understanding is a skill or ability that may be improved through training, I have argued that understanding is a form of knowledge, knowledge of the concept of understanding expressed by the word "understand" and the ability to use that concept in ascribing understanding to oneself and others. Specifically, it is learning the *sense* of the word "understand" and, second, learning the conditions to be met in ascribing understanding and justifying the ascription by appeal to reason and evidence.

The specialized study of comprehension monitoring was motivated, in part, by the discovery that students' understanding of texts was often very limited (National Center for Education Statistics, 2010). Under the banner of "accountability," the US Policy document, No Child Left Behind (NCLB), schools were required to compete in terms of objective, that is, measurable outcomes. Objective measures of comprehension also figure prominently in the American government policy document on reading and learning to read the National

Assessment of Educational Progress (NAEP) (https://nces.ed.gov/
nationsreportcard/reading/). In the attempt to make clear what was
meant by comprehension, the document enumerated a set of "basic
skills" including "phonemic awareness, phonics knowledge, fluency,
and understanding of word meanings or vocabulary" (p. 4). Clearly,
such basic skills have little or nothing to do with what is meant by
"understanding." Understanding, I have argued, is the state one is in
when one's reckoning of an expression meets the conditions of correctness and intersubjectivity. Teachers ascribe understanding to students if, in the judgment of the experts, the students have met the
criteria and students are taught how to judge the adequacy of their
own understanding. Although further research is needed, it may be
argued that the education of understanding involves learning to justify
claims of understanding by appeal to relevant evidence and reasons.

I regard it a serious weakness of the NAEP recommendations
that the question of what comprehension means is replaced by a list of
measurable skills that are correlated with understanding. One consequence of the misrepresentation is that the list of possible correlates
on offer is limited, excluding, for example, measures of composition.
Written composition, I would argue, is closely related to comprehension monitoring because they require similar judgments. Another is
that it fails to address how understanding interacts with decoding
letters to sounds. Yet this limiting approach to comprehension continues to serve as a guide to education and education research.
Furthermore, the subjective dimension of understanding emphasized
by Bruner as indexed by engagement, interest, believability, what
I called "making sense" to the reader, the very things that keep a
reader reading, are not easily captured in a set of objective written
tests and consequently play no part in the measurement of comprehension. Ironically, successful students, conscious of what matters to
them, namely test scores, often set aside their concern with understanding and ask "Will it be on the test?" before they begin their study
(Olson, 2003, p. ix) and substitute memorization for understanding.

My suggestion, then, is that comprehension monitoring is a matter of learning how to ascribe understanding to oneself and others. Once it is acknowledged that the ascription of understanding is a speech act, a matter of giving one's word for the ascription, it becomes clear that the ascriber is responsible for justifying the ascription by appeal to evidence and reason. That is, it is knowledge of the criteria for ascription of understanding and the kinds of evidence that can justify the ascription that makes understanding a rational process. It is this rationality that comprehension monitoring tasks require. If so, monitoring is intrinsic to understanding.

In my view, comprehension monitoring should be seen as a rational activity of ascription justified by evidence and reason rather than a skill to be decomposed into trainable subskills. It seems likely that student's reading competence could be improved by making clear that understanding is a concept ascribable when certain conditions have been met. Knowing what it means to understand, that is, the ability to ascribe understanding appropriately, is a worthy educational objective in its own right. The concept of understanding – like that of thinking, believing, knowing, guessing, meaning, doubting, inferring, implying, and the like – are best exemplified by means of actual literary or academic texts rather than simply defined (Murphy, 1990). Defining such terms is epistemological housekeeping, a tidying up. Yet knowledge of the concept of understanding and its relations to remembering and knowing may direct listeners and readers to "pay attention to the very words" and their interpretive contexts. Thus, in my view, comprehension monitoring is just what ascribing understanding requires.

RAISING THE LEVEL OF STUDENT READING COMPREHENSION (RFU)

While every school and every teacher is devoted to raising the literacy level of students, and every year of schooling adds to that level, since the passage of the education reform bill No Child Left Behind (NCLB

<www2.ed.gov/nclb/landing.jhtml>), there has been a concerted effort by state and national governments (not only in the United States) to raise the levels of achievement, currently deemed unsatisfactory, both by bringing advances in scientific research to bear on the design of pedagogical practices and by encouraging large-scale programs to discover "what works" in bringing about desired effects. The most recent report of such research comes from a National Academy of Education (US) report entitled *Reaping the Rewards of the Reading for Understanding Initiative* (Pearson, Palincsar, Biancarosa, & Berman, 2020). Reading for Understanding (RfU) was a massive project involving more than 1,000 researchers and practitioners in six primary research sites that adopted two worthy goals, advancing the science of "comprehension" and improving the reading comprehension ability of schoolchildren, as they put it, "to move the needle." That is, although children's reading and understanding does improve each year over the school years, the standard achieved by graduates has remained much the same over decades of educational reforms. "Moving the needle" is extremely difficult. A reading of the history of such large-scale reform efforts (Lagemann, 2000; Olson, 1975, 2003) could have alerted researchers to the hazard of such an undertaking. "Man on the moon" style phantasies about improving education are not without precedent. The report makes no reference to this branch of educational research.

The panel's own review of the research leading up to the RfU project is enlightening. The authors point out that Reading First, a massive implementation of the proposals laid out by the National Reading Panel, that emphasized decoding, phonics, word knowledge, and fluency, produced local effects but failed to enhance comprehension generally. "The failure to find any effect of Reading First on reading comprehension was, of course, a disappointing outcome considering the $6 billion investment that RF represented" (p. 21).

A second round of such research, namely Reading Next, another massive Carnegie Corporation project directed primarily at adolescent literacy comprehension, moved away from the supposed subskills of reading such as decoding to more direct attempt to improve the comprehension process by teaching comprehension strategies, including vocabulary, inferencing ability, and comprehension monitoring. Students improved on the functions taught, but the effect on student reading comprehension is unclear. When evaluated by a program "Striving Readers Comprehensive Literacy," the effects of such training were unimpressive. Of the ten interventions studied, six had no discernible effects, and the remaining four had mixed effects (p. 25). The author ruefully comments, "These findings prefigure outcomes of the RfU studies" (p. 25).

Despite this somewhat grim record, the US Institute of Education Sciences allocated some $120 million to six educational research institutions in a collaborative effort to bring the best available science to remedy the perceived shortfall of student reading comprehension. The report of this venture offers many suggestions and produced many local effects, but the goal of advancing student comprehension remains as elusive as that reported earlier in the "Striving Readers Comprehensive Literacy" program. As Paul Goodman once said, "Great advances in agronomy, but no increase in potatoes."

I consider two implications of the findings of this report: One, the fact that the practical goal of improving comprehension by applying recent cognitive science was largely unsuccessful suggests that the goal itself should be reconsidered. Second, and more serious, it is not clear that the science of "comprehension" itself has advanced by treating comprehension as a bundle of putatively distinct basic skills distinguished from reading and writing and from other manifestations of intelligence. The alternative I propose would be to take more seriously what we mean by understanding and examining what is involved in ascribing understanding, especially ascribing understanding to oneself.

On the first point, the difficulty of moving the needle, Marianne Wolf's recent book *Reader Come Home* (2018) is relevant. She noted that the average reading level of high school graduates may have plateaued or even declined as a consequence of changes in the forms and uses of reading both at home and at school. Wolf pointed out the absence of deep, sustained reading by young people, adding that this is a result of a shift in their interests to multimedia and the Internet. It is commonly agreed that people become good readers by doing a lot of reading and study of diverse texts representing the diverse genres and disciplines (Nagy, Herman & Anderson, 1985). Raising the basic reading level of a whole society is rather like raising the growth rate of the economy. Nobel Laureate Robert Solow is quoted as saying, "In real life it is very hard to move the permanent growth rate; and when it happens... the source can be a bit mysterious even after the fact" (Easterly, 2009).

On the second point, RfU brings into question whether research on understanding itself has advanced even with this massive investment of money and talent. Most accounts of understanding texts acknowledge, as Kintsch (1998) pointed out, that understanding language is a product of coordinating the properties of a text with the prior beliefs of the reader to form a model of what the reader takes the text to mean. The model of comprehension advanced in RfU, on the other hand, begins with the unpromising assumption that reading consists of decoding plus comprehension, with separate, definable skills composed of a set of similarly ersatz subskills as word knowledge, fluency, self-regulation, inhibitory control, inferencing, the ability to connect textual knowledge with prior knowledge, to monitor understanding, and so on. Unsurprisingly, such measures are all correlated with each other as well as with tests of comprehension and reading ability. This would seem to confirm the opinion of the editor of the 1924 edition of Locke's *Essay*, that understanding involves all aspects of intelligence. Furthermore, the "Striving readers" project, included in the report, found little evidence that training on a collection of such skills had a significant impact on measures of reading comprehension. In my view, the researcher's error occurred in cleaving decoding from understanding, reading from comprehension and composition from comprehension. This, of course, goes back to

Russell's and my claim that decoding and understanding are one; reading is the attempt to see the text in the light of what one believes or assumes to be true (see Chapter 4). Primary explanatory factors in understanding a text are the beliefs and commitments of the reader, their knowledge of the topic, and their linguistic and discourse knowledge. Dividing understanding into subskills seems to have gotten us no closer to what we mean by understanding than the comprehension tests gave us in the first place.

There are some suggestions in the RfU volume that perhaps comprehension is a holistic process rather than the product of simpler mental processes, and, indeed, some doubt that comprehension is a specific, trainable skill that may be measured against a fixed objective standard, although those reservations are not pursued. What is holistic about understanding, I suggest, is the concept of understanding, that is, learning the criteria for correct ascription of understanding. Although correctness and intersubjectivity are necessary conditions for understanding, ascribing or judging understanding requires that one know the criteria for understanding and knowing what could serve as evidence and reason justifying that ascription. As I put it, understanding is a rational process.

As I have argued elsewhere, attention to the properties of language that may be appealed to in justifying the ascription of understanding is greatly enhanced in learning to write and to "speak a written language" (Olson, 1994). "Thinking for writing," as Slobin (2003) pointed out, requires special attention to lexical and grammatical choice, managing anaphora, maintaining coherence, avoiding misleading expressions, anticipating objections, and the like. Comprehension monitoring is a matter of learning to read as if one were a writer. If so, comprehension and comprehension monitoring can be seen as the converse side of written composition. Both must meet the demands of decontextualization, anonymity, dictionary definitions, and reader skepticism as Corey (2020) pointed out.

Although the RfU project did not discuss the relationship between written composition and comprehension monitoring, it did report some complimentary evidence on revising texts. Students with higher levels of competence with (written) academic language were more likely to attempt to repair their understandings of text than students with lower academic language skills (p. 52). As mentioned earlier, Francis's (2019) examination of the relationship between language and literacy in a Mexican bilingual community found that students who scored higher on a test of metalinguistic awareness would revise their written texts at the phonological, semantic, and grammatical levels.

Repairs and corrections have been observed in the speech of young children (Tunmer & Herriman, 1984), and even the youngest children display an array of pointing, shrugging, and asking for clarification that suggest some awareness of the limitations of their own knowledge and understanding and that others may provide the needed information (Harris, 2020). It is not clear how this early competence is related to the linguistic awareness called for in written composition and in critically reading a text. The latter involves not only an awareness that something is amiss but also recognizing the source of the problem. Such knowledge is elaborated through an extended literate, that is, book-based education with a continued emphasis on correctness. Highly literate parents, of course, bring the school into the home by asking such questions as "What do you mean?"

Learning to meet the more demanding standards for understanding may alter the feeling of understanding as well. That is to say, children's feelings of understanding may come to be evoked by meeting the very conditions for understanding articulated by the teacher. As Proust (2014) argued, feelings continue to provide information in terms of relevance, convincingness, appealingness, and the like, which go beyond truth and correctness because the latter are grounded in one's emotional well-being. Children could be asked not only if they understand but also how they know and if they are sure.

Comprehension monitoring research focuses on self-monitoring more than monitoring the understanding of others. It remains to be explored if students can learn to self-monitor by judging whether someone else understands or not and then to diagnose what went wrong as in the Robinson, Goelman and Olson (1983) study. As I argued earlier, ascribing understanding to oneself may be short-circuited to simple confirmation of belief. Ascribing to others requires that the criteria become explicit and the evidence relevant to the judgment be available. If so, ascription to others is more important pedagogically than self-ascription. To accuse someone else of misunderstanding, as opposed to simply disagreeing, requires that the critic point to the feature of text or context that led to the misjudgment. Hence the importance of discussion with others as to the meaning of what is read.

READING AND UNDERSTANDING

The model of comprehension and comprehension monitoring discussed previously is also employed in Seidenberg's (2017) theory of reading. This shared assumption follows from what Gough (1983) called the Simple View of Reading (SVO). It is the view that reading could be considered in terms of the subskills mentioned earlier in this chapter: namely, decoding and understanding. As children already know how to understand language, all that remains to be learned, it was argued, is the skill of decoding from print to speech. Consequently, reading could be defined as decoding. Decoding was essentially phonetics, learning the sound values for letters, sometimes called "the alphabetic principle." Understanding came later.

This distinction between reading and understanding is pervasive in experimental studies of reading. Seidenberg (2017) uncritically adopted the notion that phonics is independent of and precedes understanding, claiming, "A child who has gained a basic understanding of the relation between print and sound (i.e. Phonics) can get on with the task of learning to read words" (p. 123). He granted that "[t]he insight that writing could represent speech was an epochal event in human history." Yet he went on to assert that "we aren't obligated to use that information when we read" (p. 124). We could, for example, read *Jabberwocky*! On the contrary, not only does writing represent speech but also any speech can be represented in writing. It is grasping that equivalence that makes learning to read possible. Of course, most children learn this from hearing books read to them long before they learn to read. Children have to realize that the stream of speech can be analyzed into components that can be represented by written marks and, conversely, that written marks are clues for what may be said. Only then can one work out the mapping between visual signs and spoken utterances.

Seidenberg's assumption plays out in a second way. By ignoring what children know about language by virtue of being a speaker, he can begin his analysis of reading by focusing on the properties of the text itself and treat reading as learning what texts say. His account, we could say, is text centered. Seidenberg directed much of his invective at Frank Smith (1971), whose theory of reading was, at the time, radical in that it approached reading by asking what readers, by way of their prior knowledge and expectancies, brought to the text. Smith claimed that what they saw in a text depended upon prior knowledge and experience. Children already knew what was likely to be said and they could use this to expect what is likely to be read. Smith's theory of reading was very much a part of the cognitive perspective I elaborated in Chapter 2, and it draws additional support from contemporary research in ML that provides a demonstration of the power of expectancies in seeing and reading. The point is that any stimulus is seen in the light of what one already knows.

Seidenberg did not explicitly deny expectancies but attributed them to the stimulus as if the word-familiarity effect was a property of the word itself. In fact, familiarity is just expectation, and familiar words are indeed more easily identified than unfamiliar words.

Seidenberg adopted the widely shared "dual route" model of reading, namely that in an alphabetic orthography, written signs provide both phonological and morphological information, that is, clues to both sound and meaningful units, such as words. Individual letters represent phonemes, but letters, especially strings of letters, are "orthographic clues," to the identity of words. But he then went on to dismiss the relevance of morphological cues (essential to word recognition) while claiming that phonetic clues are primary. He reviewed abundant evidence that decoding – learning the relationship between graphemes and phonemes – is the knowledge most lacking in beginning and poor readers and that teachers fail in not teaching about that relationship.

My interview with a recent graduate of one such program confirms Seidenberg's alarm that teacher education programs say nothing about language awareness, let alone phonological awareness or the importance of teaching phonics, and, indeed, guessing is treated as an alternative to learning the alphabet. However, those facts, though important, do not show that decoding is primary and independent of comprehension.

One of the problems is that whole-word recognition, that is, morphological reading, is not well understood. It is obvious that written numerals (1, 2, 3) and the dollar sign ($) are morphological signs. In reading such signs, one is reading morphologically in that no phonological clues are given by the sign and yet they are easily read. Alphabetic signs, too, may be read morphologically. The importance of the morphological route as opposed to phonological route for word identification became more obvious when reading theory attempted to account for learning to read scripts other than alphabets that have written signs that are uniquely morphological as well as signs for phonemes such as in the case of written Chinese (Chen & Pasquarella, 2017).

Seidenberg capitalized on a peculiar fact about alphabets. Only with an alphabet is it even possible to read without meaning, as in the case of *Jabberwocky* or in reading aloud an alphabetic script for an unknown language. As Share (2014) pointed out, printed words represent both units of meaning, morphemes (essentially words), and units of sound, phonemes. Morpheme-level representations are essential to rapid reading, while phonemes, represented by letters, are essential to recognizing new words. The latter presents difficulty to many beginning readers, and systematic instruction is often essential. Once children recognize the sound values for letters, they can essentially teach themselves to read. Share (2014, p. 3), who studied a range of writing systems, pointed out that morpheme distinctiveness and morpheme consistency "are crucial for rapid silent reading." He further pointed out that teachers do not teach children how to read; rather, they teach children how to teach themselves to read by providing information about the systematics of the writing system.

Although Seidenberg acknowledged that there are two routes to word identification, he insisted that "the initial hurdle is grasping the alphabetic principle," that is, the grapheme–phoneme relationship. I would say, it is the second, admittedly the most challenging hurdle, made more difficult by ignoring the prior and simpler way of recognizing a word as an orthographic unit. While he acknowledged that learning letters and their associated sounds is interactive, namely that learning letters is a route to phonological awareness, he denied that the two routes to word recognition are also interactive. In my view, recognizing that a letter string may represent a word is the first step. The second is recognizing that the letter string indicates the phonemes of the word (Ehri & Wilce, 1980).

Seidenberg's emphasis on decoding followed from Gough's sharp and misleading distinction between decoding and comprehension. The relationship is not an if-then temporal or causal relationship but rather a class-inclusive relationship: Decoding is in the service of word recognition and comprehension. In scanning letter strings, one looks for recognizable units, known words. In scanning sentences, one looks for plausible beliefs. Put another way, the scanning of letters stops when one finds a known word; the scanning of words stops when one recognizes a possible belief.

Recognizing words is the key to skilled reading. But this in no way discounts the importance of the ability to decode print into sound and to use sound to work out words one does not immediately recognize, as Seidenberg emphasized. The ability to go from letters to sounds is essential for many words and for all new words, as well as for learning to write and spell. Once one decodes an unfamiliar letter string into a known word, the letter string on a subsequent occasion may be recognized orthographically as a whole word. Morpheme recognition permits rapid reading as Share claimed.

Seidenberg's commitment to phonics led him to disparage English spellings in which the relationship between graphemes and phonemes is one to many rather than one to one. He doesn't consider the possibility that many of the most familiar words such as *have* and *some* may have irregular spellings for good reason, namely to encourage whole word recognition of "closed class" words. Seidenberg saw such irregular spellings as an impediment to reading in that such words may interfere with learning the regularities in phonics. In my view, only those children schooled on phonetics independently of known words find such spellings confusing. Indeed, people of my generation who were taught by the look-say method have difficulty in even seeing such words as irregular! What is missing is a clearer analysis of how making sense interacts with learning to decode. This, of course, is the same problem we encountered in accounting for the role of belief in understanding.

A cognitive view that takes seriously the premise that experience is taken up in terms of the already known would reverse the decoding plus understanding formula and insist that children expect that what they encounter in print makes sense and, hence, that attempts at making sense precede and are critical to decoding. In fact, the general impression of the book is that Seidenberg never grasped the basic principle of the "cognitive revolution," namely that prior beliefs affect perception, the basic assumption of the view that Seidenberg rejected.

Seidenberg (2017) claimed to have provided important evidence from current research on reading that demonstrates the inadequacy of Smith's prediction theory. In fact, the interesting research he summarized offers little of relevance to the nature of reading or the nature of understanding beyond showing that knowledge of grapheme–phoneme relations is important and lacking especially in poor readers. But poor readers are not only poor at decoding. They are also poor at prediction, inference, and comprehension generally. Correlations amongst such variables imply that reading ability is a general ability, a fact well captured by the move of treating reading along with writing as components of literacy as exemplified by the Whole Language movement.

Learning to read and learning to read critically both involve the ascription of understanding to oneself and others and could offer a new framework for further research.

13 Understanding in Everyday Life

Both academic research and educational theory set a lofty standard of correctness for understanding and may differ from that honored in ordinary language and political discourse. It is argued that the concept of understanding is general, but the weight given to prior beliefs and commitments affects the evidence a listener or reader picks up from the text. This view is examined in the context of rational reasoning tasks and political discourse.

To this point I have offered an account of understanding by examining the conditions under which one can correctly and appropriately ascribe understanding to oneself or another. Correctness, I argued, depends on honoring the evidence available from an expression or text. Intersubjectivity is achieved by bringing the beliefs of the speaker and listener into alignment. These beliefs and expectations were left relatively unanalyzed, sometimes simply glossed as "context." What calling this background the context fails to acknowledge is the depth of the beliefs and commitments that subjects bring to their understanding, commitments so fundamental that the linguistic properties of an expression are neglected. This is one implication of the proposition that all understanding involves the fixation and updating of beliefs; understanding is never the sentence processing independent of these beliefs.

It remains to be seen if this simple scheme accounts for the diversity of persons and contexts in which understanding is assumed to take place. I have argued that understanding is a single phenomenon is represented by the concept of understanding that one may ascribe to self or others. I shall examine how this account applies in two quite different contexts, the study of reasoning and in political discourse.

Ascribing understanding sets a somewhat lofty goal in that one must judge that understanding has been achieved and that judgment can be made only by appeal to evidence and reason for the ascription. When a teacher ascribes or claims that a student has failed to understand, they must indicate the property of the expression that could remedy the misunderstanding. Ordinary understanding, on the other hand, meets the conditions for understanding, namely correctness and intersubjectivity but, unless challenged, does not require that the understander provide reason or evidence for correctness. Ordinarily discourse flows without much attention to either of these critical features. Not only are a speaker's expressions attuned to the expectancies of the listener, failure to reach agreement may be resolved by further interaction.

On other occasions, a common understanding may not be achieved, and the parties may accuse each other of ignorance, bigotry, or misunderstanding. Ascribing misunderstanding like ascribing understanding is a claim about correctness that can be resolved by pointing to the relevant evidence. Claims of ignorance, irrationality, or bigotry cannot be so resolved.

Consequently, understanding may be ascribed to a person or system independently of whether that person or system ascribes understanding to itself. This is what I earlier called "ascribe to." Young children understand simple expressions when they meet the conditions for understanding even if they lack the ability to ascribe understanding. Adults, too, understand expressions quite independently of whether they self-ascribe understanding or justify their understanding by appeal to evidence. Recall the ascription is an assertion that one understands, a claim that must be justified by evidence and reason. Thus, there is a burden on the ascriber that is not required of the one to whom understanding is ascribed.

REASONING AS UNDERSTANDING

Understanding the expressions used in formal reasoning tasks make essentially the same demands as the expressions used in comprehension monitoring tasks and in the school. Such tasks pit straightforward understanding with the self-ascription of understanding. The latter requires justifying the claim that one understands by appeal to reasons and evidence. Subjects read a story, understanding it in a way that makes sense to them. The expert then points out some evidence that shows that the subjects had actually failed to understand and are encouraged to revise their understanding. To succeed on such school-like tasks, the subject must learn to read the story in the way that the expert does, namely to see if the ascription of understanding is warranted. The reader has to not only understand but also ascribe understanding to himself or herself. Ascription, as I argued, is a claim about understanding justifiable by appeal to the evidence available in the story or text.

Consider again Kahneman's (2011) account of the fact that adults often draw invalid inferences from statements. That is, subjects claim that they understand, but the experimenter claims that they did not understand. In one widely cited example, the so-called Linda problem, subjects are told:

> Linda is thirty-one years old, single, outspoken and very bright. She majored in philosophy. As a student, she was deeply concerned with issues of discrimination and social justice, and also participated in antinuclear demonstrations.

Subjects were then asked: Which alternative is more probable?

(1) Linda is a bank teller, or
(2) Linda is a bank teller and is active in the feminist movement.

Subjects reliably choose (2). However, strictly speaking, (1) is more probable in that (2) is a subset of (1). For example, it is more likely that one is a man than that one is a young man. So why do subjects choose (2)? The correct answer hangs critically on the term "probable" that the experimenter and a few more highly educated and statistically proficient subjects base their choice of (1) on. Ordinary readers may be less attentive to the precise meaning of "probable" and base their answer on other aspects of the story that make (2) plausible.

Kahneman's task is basically a "bait and switch" task in that it is designed to mislead readers in order to demonstrate that people's reasoning is not strictly rational but based rather on strategic "heuristics" and "biases," that is, the reader's beliefs and expectations as to what is likely to be the case. Of course, biases were precisely what the cognitive revolution established, namely that what is perceived is perceived in the light of what is known. Kahneman induced these biases and expectations in the early part of the story and they lead readers to errors in judgment. These biases demonstrate the priority of one's beliefs and expectancies in the uptake of any linguistic expression and demonstrate the validity of Kahneman's claim that reasoning is not always not strictly rational.

However, one may ask if Kahneman's subjects are irrational in picking (2). Kahneman assumed that the two facts about Linda, namely that she was a feminist and that she was a banker, are independent. However, it may be argued that in a narrative context, the stated facts are not seen as independent. In a story, the first sentence is often treated as the topic or theme of the following discourse. Kahneman's Linda story does this, inadvertently, by providing a theme for the story in terms of which Linda is portrayed as a socially conscious activist. Any new information must be fitted into the frame set by the topic sentence. Thus, the second fact, that she became a banker, must be set within the frame of her social consciousness that introduced the story. As Chekhov pointed out – the so-called Chekhov's Law – if a gun is introduced in the first act, it must be fired in the third. To achieve this integration, Kahneman's subjects appear to nudge the word "probable" to its less-statistical cousin "plausible" and conclude that it is likely that Linda is both a feminist and a banker.

Did subjects "understand"? An expert would say no, because they failed to honor the strict meaning of "probable." But did they understand the story? Yes, because they managed to make something whole out of the story fragments. Hence, the adults studied by Kahneman are like the five-year-olds who agreed that some elephants have trunks. They both managed to fit what they heard into what they could plausibly believe. They felt they understood even if they did not meet the adult, objective criteria for ascribing understanding. Those who did succeed with Kahneman's task could not only understand but also ascribe understanding to themselves and justify their understanding by appeal to the linguistic evidence available to everyone.

Kahneman called the two strategies fast and slow, the former unreflective and the other more deliberate. Stanovich (2009) distinguished them as irrational and rational. I describe them as understanding as opposed to ascribing understanding. The advantage of my account is that it appeals only to the concept of understanding and the speaker's role in ascribing the concept.

POLITICAL RHETORIC

Ivan Illich (1991) offered the concept of lay literacy, the knowledge of language that nonspecialists picked up within a literate society without actually becoming "scholarly." For the "educated," more precisely, the highly educated, understanding often meets standard for ascribing understanding, that is, for making a justifiable claim about understanding. Laypersons, nonspecialists may understand but not take the second step of ascribing understanding to themselves and of justifying their understanding by an exhaustive examination of the linguistic or contextual evidence. Failure to do so is greeted by their more literary critics as irrational (Stanovich, 2009).

For many people, and perhaps for all people under some circumstances, what they read or hear makes sense – it comports with plausible beliefs – even if the conditions for ascription of understanding are not met. Often, it doesn't matter. A familiar television series entitled *Impossible Railways* goes on to show that the railway has actually been built. How then can such railways be said to be impossible? Similarly, in Diane Setterfield's *Once Upon A River*, a character plausibly exclaims, "Just [be]cause a thing is impossible, don't mean it can't happen" to which his listener nods agreement. The charm of Setterfield's story is that she and her readers recognize an irony presumably unrecognized by the characters themselves.

While all understanding depends on prior knowledge, vernacular understanding may give undue weight to prior beliefs and commitments, the biases discussed by Kahneman. This becomes clear in the case of political rhetoric where the beliefs and biases of audiences overwhelmingly determine how any expression is understood. This is being written at the time when political discourse, especially in the United States, has become increasingly polemical and in a sense tests the limits of any theory of understanding.

Political rhetoric is peculiar in that it is speech addressed to believers. Political rhetoric, like religious rhetoric, is designed for the already converted. It is an expression of shared hopes and desires rather than a report of objective truth, a language of solidarity rather than argument, of invitation to action rather than to reflection. For believers, political rhetoric is not recognized as polemical; it is seen as expressing obvious truths. Thus, to the alarm of the "scholarly," Trump and his many followers claimed not only to understand such expressions as "stop the steal," "fake news," "voter fraud," and the like but also to take them as expressions of a deeper truth.

Rhetorical speech is not always recognized for what it is. The problem became acute when then president Trump actually put his rhetorical speech into written form on Twitter. Once written down, such statements are assumed to have taken on the form of objective claims and so are rejected by nonbelievers as hyperbole, distortions, and outright lies. That is, nonbelievers read the written expressions on Twitter as they would read any other serious written document of the type that would be acceptable in law, government, or the academy. Critics employing these conventions for written documents treat them as evidence that Trump's rhetorical expressions are false. Trump's believers, however, continue to take them as truth. So who understands? Believers can accept them as true; nonbelievers reject them for failing to meet the academic norms for written documents.

These two audiences react in dramatically different ways. Political analysts noted a demographic feature that distinguished two classes of voters as the "educated" and the "less educated," the latter referring to Trump voters. Although a majority of both groups have a high school education, it has been noted that Trump and his supporters are not habitual book and newspaper readers but rely more on social media, public rallies, and face-to-face interaction. Habitual readers are more familiar with the language of law, justice, science, and serious literature, a language appropriate equally to believers and nonbelievers. This type of language meets the standards for the ascription of understanding, namely expressions designed to meet the standards for correctness and intersubjectivity and designed equally for believers and skeptics.

A common response of the educated elite familiar with academic language is to regard Trump and his followers as irrational and to proffer a systematic education as the only solution. Education is charged with teaching everyone to master the literate norms of objective discourse in which evidence and reason carry the day. Modern societies charge the school with the task of bringing everyone up to a certain literate standard, and, as we saw in Chapter 12, schools are often accused of failing to deliver on this charge.

There was a time when it seemed possible to set and enforce rules for the correct use of language. In the seventeenth century, the French Academy attempted to set out standards for the correct use of language and created the *ecoles normales* to teach children to honor those rules. Jonathan Swift made similar proposals for the reform of English. Nebrija, a fifteenth-century grammarian, also recommended to Queen Isabella that she impose clear rules for language, as the speech of common people was seen as "loose and unruly." The queen rejected the advice, claiming that language was a common possession of the people, not just of experts and authorities (Illich & Sanders, 1989, p. 65). Modern societies turn to education to achieve through training what cannot be achieved by regulation. Indeed, a recent report (Lee, White & Dong, 2021) prepared for the US National Academy of Education (NAEd) offers an urgent proposal for improving the civic reasoning and discourse of students.

But, alas, it is too late. It is impossible to impose academic norms on adults who exult in the freedom of speech. In a democracy, all citizens, not only the highly literate, have a right to be heard and a right to vote. The alternative is to admit that for many adults, the language of thought is largely rhetorical, shaped for believers, and not that of the academy, shaped for skeptics. The question is how to understand polemical language if we are not to simply dismiss it as irrational. What the "educated" have yet to learn is to understand rhetorical language not as irrational but as an expression of more basic, inchoate feelings and beliefs that must be addressed at some point.

Language ability is a small part of the problem. The basic problem is the weight of prior beliefs and commitments in the understanding of any expression. If what is heard comports with one's basic beliefs, it is easily accepted; if it violates or seems to violate those beliefs, it is rejected whether one heard every word or not. Loeb (2021), a media consultant, pointed out that media campaigns fail because "data-driven persuasion is generally limited to leveraging existing biases" and are ineffective in overturning existing beliefs. Rather than challenging the preconceptions and biases of opponents, it may be more promising to take their concerns seriously and, if possible, address them. Dismissing opponent's concerns as irrational will only infuriate them and reduce any willingness to continue discussion.

Consequently, rhetorical expressions should not be ignored as irrational but rather as sincere expressions of deeply felt needs and desires. The rationality of rhetorical expressions may be seen by recognizing as equally rhetorical the expression "Black lives matter." This too is a call to action enforced by protest. To believers, the expression is greeted as a factual claim but rejected by skeptics as a tautology. Rather than denying the importance of sincerely held feelings simply because they are rhetorical, one could get down to a more basic discussion of what one wants and acknowledge that arguments and evidence perceived as running contrary to those deeper wants and convictions will be denied or ignored. As I pointed out earlier, understanding without believing is difficult and, if the beliefs are deeply felt, impossible. It may be more useful to encourage people to know and honor what we mean by understanding with its conditions of correctness and intersubjectivity. This would seem to be an achievable educational goal.

Illich's (1991) concept of lay literacy highlighted the difference between being informed and being "scholarly." For the highly educated, the language of thought tends to be more relentlessly academic in that it depends on precise use of language suited to law and government and for reading literature what is referred to as the written register. For ordinary citizens, the language of thought is tailored to preserving belief. Even for the scholarly, prior beliefs are not easily set aside. Societies have yet to learn how to negotiate across these notions of what it means to understand.

A comparable division has emerged in Canada where a new recognition of the rights of Aboriginal people leads to possible conflicts between the documented views of highly literate bureaucrats and the views of tribal chiefs of indigenous cultures for whom oral traditional knowledge is carried by the elders and claims are supported by tradition and environmental signs as much as by written documents. It is now widely acknowledged that modern societies made a serious error in thinking of such societies as primitive or irrational just because beliefs tended to be communal rather than documented. And there is now considerable optimism that disputes may be resolved not only by argument but also by taking competing concerns seriously.

The very nature of agreement is problematic. According to a recent account (Mason, Globe, & Mail, March 5, 2021), the Government of Canada negotiated an agreement with the hereditary chiefs giving them title over Wet'suwet'en territory. Many still don't know what exactly is stated in the agreement. The chiefs hold ownership over the information and have been unwilling to share this information or to document, put into writing, the oral agreement. The issues remain unresolved. The meanings to be expressed are not easily captured in the language of written law. And deeply held faith is not easy to articulate.

It is unreasonable to ask or expect that the standards for valid literate argument in achieving understanding will be set aside as irrelevant. Nevertheless, it should also be acknowledged that not everyone is skilled in giving valid reasons for their beliefs. While education is critical to valid argument, it is neither universal nor completely successful. What is universal and not reliant on a higher education is the rhetorical language that can be recognized as an expression of what people value, desire, and fear whether the expression meets impeccable literate standards or not. Discourse across cultures may have to accommodate what makes sense to both parties, to be followed, if necessary, by crafting words that both parties can assent to even while believing somewhat different things. It matters less if one believes that a policy derives from universal Kantian principles or from common sense so long as participants can agree on the desired observable outcomes. Truths, as Taylor put it, are not only true but must seem to be true.

14 Ascriptivism and Cognitive Development

> In this chapter, I describe how our understanding of children's minds may be reformulated by asking how we ascribe mental states, such as belief and understanding, to them. Children's developing ability to ascribe those states to themselves and others offers a possible explanation of the origin of rational, self-conscious, and introspectable mental states.

In the first chapter of this book, I contrasted the first-order subjective experience of understanding, the "A ha!" experience of making sense, with the objective valid ascription of understanding that had long been the concern of analytical philosophers. I sought to bring the first-person experience and the third-person ascription together into one account of understanding.

FEELINGS

In retrospect, it has become clear that the "A ha" experience I described as a first-person subjective experience is not simply a first-person subjective experience. In fact, it is both experienced and avowed, the first a subjective feeling, the second an objectively evaluable truth claim about that state. Thus, the subjective experience of understanding and its avowal are quite different things. An avowal is a self-ascription possible only for one who has knowledge of the concept of understanding. The feeling of understanding is not an essential feature of the concept of understanding. The relevance of the feeling of understanding is justified in another way, namely as the degree of certainty associated with any understanding. Introspection of one's mind is self-ascription, the application to the self of the mental state designated by a linguistic concept.

Ascriptions of understanding and other mental states are possible because of the availability of the necessary language; they are sayables. To be acquired as a part of an ordinary language, the concept must be sharable and public. To repeat what now seems obvious although it took a Wittgenstein to point it out, there is no private language for thinking. Only a public language has a standard for correctness, the point contested by Humpty Dumpty in his well-known argument with Alice as to his right to make words mean whatever he wanted.[1]

Feelings, such as the subjective feeling of understanding, have no socially shared standard of correctness. Consequently, one can feel they understand when, if fact, they misunderstand. Rather, feelings are part of the emotional system with an immediate, experiential content conferred by the appraisal process, with predispositions for action and a phenomenal tone, a buzz or tingle. This is the system that regulates our behavior. The word or concept of understanding, on the other hand, captures only that aspect relevant to truth while setting aside the predispositions for action as well as the feeling tone. I cited Taylor and Proust as showing that feelings allow one to monitor the conceptual content in terms of valence, relevance, and certainty. Thus, understanding can be both correct and heartfelt.

The readiness for action and the phenomenal tone that are properties of the feeling are not a part of the meaning of the term. We may understand the word "grief" without feeling the pain involved or any call to sympathize. The loss of the phenomenal tone and its connection to action gives language its disembodied, abstract character, a loss that Husserl saw as the crisis of western science. At the same time, that loss is why first- and third-person ascriptions of understanding are equivalent; they meet the same standards for correctness.

The feeling of understanding may, nonetheless, contribute to the acquisition of the concept of understanding. I suggested that the

---

[1] Shades of former president Trump!

FIGURE 14.1 What it feels like
Source: Permission applied for from Scott Adams and the Andrews McMeel
Syndication, Kansas City, MO.

feeling of understanding may provide the intuition that is confirmed
by the acquisition of the concept. As I pointed out, both McGinn and
Strawson argued that one could not acquire the concept of understanding unless one had experienced the feeling of understanding.
While this may be generally true, there are counterexamples: I know
what it is to be a genius, but I don't know what it feels like (see Figure
14.1). Scott Adams's "Dilbert" cartoon shows a defeated-looking
businessman saying, "I wonder what it feels like to win?" to which
his avatar replies, "It feels great!"[2]

SENSES AS CONCEPTS

The clear distinction between the feeling of understanding and the
concept of understanding allowed me to raise the more specific

---

[2] As this was going to press, I came across a quotation from painter Lucian Freud: "I
long to have what I imagine natural talent felt like" (New Yorker, February 8, 2021,
p. 66).

question as to the "identity conditions" for the feeling and to contrast them with the identity conditions for the concept of understanding. Those critical for the concept of understanding, I argued, were truth or correctness on one hand and intersubjectivity on the other. Only then did it become clear that the identity conditions for the concept of understanding were identical to those for the word "understand." That is, the conditions to be met in identifying understanding were identical to those for the correct ascription of understanding. It is the word "understand" with a distinct *sense* or meaning that can be applied to diverse expressions, each of which meets those conditions in its own way.

The sense-reference distinction is possible only for words. A word is a phonological form with a place in grammar and with a *sense* and a reference. To learn the phonological sign "understand" with a *sense* creates a type–token relation, that is, a kind–object distinction. The sense of the word "understand" creates a category, a type, or a kind of which each instance of understanding is a token. As John Macnamara (1986) pointed out, one can only see a thing as a kind of a thing. Some will recall Piaget's (1962) early observation of his young child saying "Here's thing-a-ma-bob again" when in fact it was another one of the same kind. The concept of understanding, then, can be reduced to knowledge of the word "understand"; the meaning of the word determines the boundaries of the concept. Consequently, the question of what understanding is can be reduced or replaced by the question of what "understanding" means.

Understanding is a linguistic concept with identity conditions that must be met for the correct ascription of understanding. The primary identity conditions, I argued, are truth and intersubjectivity. The concept of understanding does not rise ostensively by learning a word to point to an existing but private concept of understanding, nor from the child's own cognitive resources such as reflective abstraction. Concepts are formed, I argued, by learning a word with phonological form and a distinctive *sense* that picks out a *reference*. That reference is the belief produced in response to the expression.

Consequently, concepts are word meanings. Understanding is just what the word "understand" means.

ASCRIBED "BY" AND ASCRIBED "TO"

Clearly, it is the knowledge of the word "understand" that permits ascription. Only older children know and use the word "understand." What then are we to make of the fact that young children, and perhaps other animals, manifestly understand expressions long before they learn the word "understand"? What is often overlooked is that it is we, adult speakers, who make ascriptions. We ascribe understanding to young children because, in our view, child's behavior meets the identity conditions for our concept, namely correctness and intersubjectivity. Similarly, we may ascribe understanding to computers if, in our judgment, they meet our criteria. The ascription is made quite independently of what those persons or objects know or feel, indeed, whether they have any feelings or knowledge at all. What the young child, other animals, or computers cannot do, I argued, is ascribe understanding to themselves or others. They lack the mutually agreed words to make the ascription. To ascribe is to make an assertion that may be true or false and for which the speaker may be held responsible. Thus, ascribing is a complex cognitive undertaking. To ascribe requires the ability to judge that understanding has indeed met the conditions for correct ascription. That judgment can be made only if one knows the criteria and the kinds of evidence that could justify the ascription. Hence, there is a fundamental difference between having understanding ascribed to one and the actual ability to make the ascription. I called this the "ascribed to" as opposed to the "ascribed by" distinction. Hence the reductive conclusion I mentioned at the outset, namely that understanding may be reduced to knowledge of how to use the word "understand."

As I wrote, in the analysis of understanding, there are only two fundamental issues. The first is to work out the identity conditions for the concept of understanding. Those turn out to be precisely those that define the *sense* of the word "understand." The second issue is to ask who is making the ascription. It is our ability, as linguistically competent adults, to ascribe understanding to all sorts of sentient beings if in our judgment they meet the identity criteria for the meaning of the word "understanding." Our ascriptions can be made quite independently of whether those creatures themselves are speakers or have a concept of understanding. Moreover, it is our ability to ascribe understanding to ourselves and others that allows us to know and to claim that we do, in fact, understand. This is what children learn when they learn to ascribe understanding. By associating the phonological form of the word with sorting out the identity conditions for the use of the word, the child, too, can acquire the ability to ascribe.

The concept (word) of understanding is applicable to self and others, but there is an important, if unacknowledged, implication of self-ascription. Self-ascription, I argue, creates the mental state. One can ascribe understanding to oneself only if the ascription is judged by reference to the identity criteria for understanding. To self-ascribe understanding correctly is all there is to the mental state of understanding. There is something that "it is like" to understand, namely the knowledge that one has met the criteria for ascription and the feeling of certainty that the ascription is appropriate.

To repeat, ascribing can be done only if one knows the conditions for the correct use of the term. One cannot be an ascriber of understanding unless one knows what is involved in meeting the conditions of correctness and intersubjectivity. On the other hand, understanding can be ascribed to systems that do not know these conditions but merely are seen as meeting them. Ascribing raises, perhaps for the first time, the need for evidence and reason for justifying the ascription.

ASCRIPTIVISM

Ascriptivism put concepts and language at the heart of cognition. Joseph Heath (personal communication) pointed out that ascriptivism was widely adopted in philosophy to avoid what was seen as the dead end of Cartesianism, that is, to avoid explanations based on postulating private, unobservable spiritual and mystical mental states. Many cognitivists have no such reluctance and have long explained the behavior of animals by attributing beliefs, cognitive maps, mental codes, and concepts to them if evidence seemed to warrant such attributions. Consequently, we cognitivists have sometimes failed to recognize the extent to which our perceptions of behavior are limited by our own linguistic resources. That is, we linguistic creatures understand ourselves and others in terms of the resources available in our own linguistic system. Given the generative resources of a natural language, this is not a limitation but a resource for bringing experience into thought.

Again, it is we ascribers who ascribe states to both linguistic and nonlinguistic creatures. But in ascribing such states to ourselves and others, we must know the criteria to be met and the evidence and reasons that would justify the ascription. When we do so in response to a linguistic expression, we experience that state as understanding. This self-reflective quality is peculiar to mental state concepts; there is something that it is like to understand. That something includes the subjective feeling of understanding, but it is the concept that is critical, as the feeling may arise both when one understands and when one thinks they understand but, in fact, misunderstand. That is why the feeling cannot provide a definition for the concept.

To see understanding as the application of the concept of understanding provides a new perspective to the psychological study of comprehension and comprehension monitoring. The focus of such studies is one of the identity conditions for the concept of understanding, namely correctness. Correctness is met through satisfying two sets of constraints: the prior knowledge of the language and the beliefs and goals of the subject in terms of which an expression is understood. I argued that prior belief and expectancy, what the subject takes as true, is primary. Consequently, what is readily believed is readily understood, and believing is easier than understanding without belief.

This reverses the conventional assumption that reading (decoding) precedes understanding. Rather, what is read is read in terms of the prior beliefs and expectancies of the reader in the attempt to preserve and update one's beliefs.

I proposed that the experimental study of comprehension and comprehension monitoring should be seen not as a skill but rather as knowledge of the identity criteria to be met and the evidence that could relevant to ascribing understanding. Hence, monitoring is not something added to understanding but rather the scrupulous, knowledgeable rational application of the identity criteria for the concept.

ASCRIPTION AND THEORY OF MIND

Astington (1996) stated succinctly what I have been attempting to defend, namely that "one only possesses a Theory of Mind when one can say that one does." Mind is not a substance as Medieval philosophers once thought and it is not a spiritual, soul-like entity as Descartes thought. As Ryle (2009) argued, there is no "ghost in the machine." Nor is understanding a mental, computational, or brain process. Rather, mind is a set of concepts that we acquire as we learn a social language applicable to what we or others say in order to distinguish successful occasions of understanding from unsuccessful ones such as misunderstanding. To learn the language of mind is to acquire a Theory of Mind. It is acquired not by reflective abstraction, decontextualization, metarepresentation, or frontal lobe processing although verbal concepts have all these features, but by learning a language. The mental states we introspect are the states that we are in when we are satisfied that we have met the identity conditions for that concept. When we understand, we not only know we understand but also feel that we do.

In acquiring language for the ascription of mental states, children become ascribers. Ascribing, as I pointed out, is an assertion or claim for which one is held accountable by others, and in this way one learns to be responsible for one's own ascriptions.

MENTAL REPRESENTATION

What we mean by understanding, and consequently what understanding is, is the linguistic knowledge that allows one to ascribe understanding and misunderstanding to oneself or another. This theory would seem to invert the psychological view that understanding is a complex mental process formed by Piagetian equilibration, concept formation, decentering, social discourse, and the like and insist, rather, that understanding is learning the definitional constraints for using the word "understand." It is the word "understand," a word in a public language, with identity conditions for its use, primary among them the notion of truth – that would allow the distinction between understanding and misunderstanding – and shareability that would allow the concept to apply equally to self and other. Moreover, obviously, it is knowledge of the word that allows ascription, a verbal practice, to ourselves or others. That is, we avow or claim to understand when we know we meet the conditions and we ascribe understanding to others when we think they do.

Reducing the concept of understanding to the meaning of the word "understand" would seem to grossly underestimate the challenge faced by a child in grasping the "identity conditions" for the correct application of a term. Meeting the criterion of truth of a belief as opposed to the criterion of success of adaptive behavior is a dramatic cognitive, stage-defining achievement. Similarly, self–other equivalence in the understanding of a word is a massive intellectual achievement that distinguishes the egocentrism of a young child's private experience from the more impersonal, decentered, view essential to word learning. We see this when children misuse words or neglect one of its defining features. Furthermore, as deVilliers (2005) has shown (Chapter 10), to attribute a false belief requires a complex grammar that incorporates both a meaning believed and a meaning merely entertained. To ascribe understanding similarly requires a complex grammar as in "I understand what you mean" even if we don't believe what you say. Consequently, ascriptivism does not negate cognitive psychology but builds on what is known, as well as what is yet to be learned, about children's cognitive and linguistic development. But it does have an unanticipated implication, namely that children do not have a mind, let alone know their own minds or recognize the minds of others until they acquire the appropriate language for mind. Knowing one's own mind, as I argued, is self-ascription.

As mentioned earlier, what I take away from preverbal children in the denial of belief and understanding to them, I give back by way of an elaborated notion of states of feeling. Feeling states are not mere tingles and buzzes but complex cognitive–emotion states with a content that accumulates with experience and provides the basis for expectation. These feeling states are composed of appraisals of situations, preparations for action, as well as their phenomenal tone. Feelings are the states of consciousness characteristic of young children, other animals, and that provide the experiential basis for all learning, including learning a language. In learning a public language, children furnish their minds with concepts and sentences with their truth bearing roles in the fixation of belief. Only a linguistic mind, I argued, has concepts and beliefs. Thoughts, as Searle (1983) put it, are essentially sincerity conditions for utterances. Or, as Vendler (1970) put it, thinking is to saying as playing the piano is to running the fingers over the keyboard but not actually pushing the keys down, yet hearing the sounds in one's mind. Sellars (1997, pp. 90–94), building on Kant's claim that "intuitions without concepts are blind," argued that "thoughts are linguistic episodes."

THE LINGUISTIC TURN IN THE THEORY OF MIND

The shift required to move from thinking of understanding as a complex set of mental processes to thinking of understanding as a concept with identity conditions for its ascription seemed to me to be momentous. Only when I realized that concepts could be explained as word meanings and that the word "understand" allowed ascription to self and other did the linguist turn seem plausible. I took heart from philosophers Wittgenstein, Heath, and Davidson, all of whom had insisted that thinking is essentially a linguistic achievement. Cognitive development, if this is true, becomes, in large part, conceptual development, a matter of learning language for talking and thinking the world and learning a language for talking and thinking about what is said. If so, conceptual development is, in large part, semantic development. Accommodating the subjective feelings of children to the demands of a public language is the story of the formation of mind. This is the picture of mind that I came to grant as I explored the concept of understanding.

Brandom's (2004, p. 6) bold and controversial assertion that "grasping a concept is mastering the use of a word" expresses succinctly just what I have been driving at in my account of what it means to understand, namely that the concept of understanding can be reduced to the mastery of the *sense* of the word "understand" and, in turn, knowing the conditions under which one, including oneself, can correctly be said to understand. One understands only when one can correctly ascribe understanding to oneself and others. Thus, understanding is both a concept and the mental state one is in when one correctly ascribes understanding to oneself.

The question is, then, why did I not begin with Brandom rather than with the study of children's mental states? The simple answer is that I read Brandom's claim as interesting but implausible. First, it seemed to put the cart before the horse; surely one had the concept and, given the opportunity, one learned how to express the concept in a public language. Second, Piaget and others had shown, had they not, that young children had all sorts of concepts and feelings that they appeared to work up quite independently of language as their intellectual resources developed. Third, young children appeared to acquire an understanding of the minds of others through play and social interaction without language. Language seemed to be only, as we said, "an expression of thought."

It was the research on children's understanding of false belief that decisively pointed to the significance of acquiring a concept of belief applicable to self and other. However, for a concept to be applicable to self and other would seem to require a public language. Hence, I concluded that there was a close link between a psychological concept and the verbal form. In fact, there is considerable evidence (reviewed in Chapter 10) that conceptual development is semantic development. Concepts and word meanings are not merely correlated but rather concepts come into existence with language. Concepts are words with a *sense* and a reference; no word, no concept. Concepts pick out and categorize their referents. Only words allow the sense-reference distinction. Preverbal cognitions make no categorical distinction between the same thing again and another one of the same kind. Although I had long granted Vygotsky's view that "[t]he word is a microcosm of human consciousness," only when I realized that concepts could be seen as words with a *sense* as distinguished from what the word referred to did Brandom's claim become plausible. Although I began my analysis with young children's pre-linguistic cognitive feelings and emotions, I was led to explain conceptual development in terms of the acquisition of language, in particular, their learning mental concepts that could be used for ascribing those states to themselves and others. When I attempted to set out the identity conditions that distinguished feelings from concepts for those states – which in cognitive developmental terms are commonly described as distinguishing features of concepts – I found that those features corresponded to the *senses* of the words used for ascribing mental states. If so, just as Brandom said, concepts are word meanings. A major part of the cognitive work that infants and young children put into building up their mental competence, then, is learning how to use a set of linguistic conventions. Putting it this way seemed to minimize the child's achievement. In fact, coordinating truth and self–other equivalence are massive cognitive achievements.

It requires an important change to psychological theorizing to see concepts as word meanings. Concepts of objects, for example, were long explained in terms of recognizing distinguishing or defining features of objects themselves. It was only with Frege (see Chapter 8) that meanings were clearly distinguished from their referents. As Bennett (1971, p. 353) pointed out, "a concept or word meaning is nothing like a quasi-sensory mental episode." Charles Dickens's pedantic pedagogue Gradgrind was ahead of his time when he insisted that "horse" be defined not by pointing to horses but by relating the word "horse" to other words such as "domesticated" and "quadraped." The feeling of understanding may be based on the reference rather than the meaning of the term "understand." The conceptual discoveries that the children make are joint products of the intuitions drawn from the appraisals involved in emotional states and the distinctions marked in the linguistic practices of adults. Whereas subjectively experienced feelings are private and personal, word knowledge is shared in a public language. However, it is only because the language can refer to objects and states in the world that they are worth learning in the first place. The word "horse" is of little use if there are no horses, nor "understanding" if there is no understanding.

LIMITATIONS OF ASCRIPTIVISM

I consider two limitations of ascriptivism as a theoretical approach to mental states. The first is its denial or exclusion of feelings. I argued that the feeling of understanding confers certainty on one's understanding. The second is that ascriptivism fails to sufficiently acknowledge that the ascription is made by someone. Ascription assumes first-person subjectivity. Consequently, it fails to distinguish ascription *to* a subject from ascription *by* a subject, for it is the latter that makes understanding a rational activity. I consider them in turn.

Ascriptivism is the attempt to explain behavior and thought in terms of concepts in a public language. Hence, ascription of understanding occludes the first-person subjective feelings of certainty and commitment to reality that are part of subjective understanding, as feelings are private. We may ascribe the feeling of understanding to one if their uptake of an expression allows them to "go on" even if they do not fully understand. Yet, as I acknowledged, feelings do not make it so; understanding implies correctness and intersubjectivity, neither of which is guaranteed by the feeling that something makes sense. For this reason, philosophers of mind are largely dismissive of subjective feelings in their accounts of knowledge and belief and rely exclusively on objective criteria.

The denial of subjective states led to important criticisms by Janack (2012) who criticized Willard Van Orman Quine and Richard Rorty for speculating about children and language learning without any attention to advances in research of children's subjectivity, intentionality, their capacity for joint attention, or their theory of mind. She argued that the retreat from a first-person perspective derives from the methodologies of behaviorism and computationalism. She reprised Bruner's theory of subjective experience and personal meaning as a possible corrective.

I attempted to balance Janack's emphasis on subjectivity with an equal emphasis on the public nature of linguistic concepts. Subjective feelings are experienced as personal and private and cannot be brought into a public language simply by pointing to them – there is no unique thing to point to prior to the concept. Davidson (2001) offered two reasons for setting aside subjective feelings and emotions in his analysis of knowledge and its acquisition. He claimed that feelings are unreliable, more often justifications for, rather than cause of, beliefs and, second, that first-person feelings are not better evidence for what one believes or understands than the kinds of evidence available to others. That is, we self-ascribe correctly when we apply the same rules to our own thoughts that we do in ascribing states to others. It seems clear that Davidson would ascribe understanding to any creature or system that meets the criteria for understanding, thus neglecting the informational use of the feeling of understanding, that is, the feeling of certainty and relevance that accompanies correct understanding.

The second limitation of ascriptivism is its failure to distinguish between "ascribe to" and "ascribe by," namely the fact that an ascription is made by someone. I introduced the distinction to account for the fact that we may correctly ascribe understanding to young children, other animals, and computers even if they, lacking the concept of understanding, cannot ascribe understanding to themselves or others. It is the concept that allows older children and adults to make the ascriptions. It is the act of ascription that matters because ascribing is a judgment that is subject to reason and evidence and can be contested on just those grounds. "Is it true?" and "Is it shareable?" are the criteria on the basis of which the judgment is to be made. Ascription, like any assertion, is something for which the ascriber must take responsibility and, indeed, will be held accountable by others.

Brandom (2009, p. 212) perhaps anticipated my distinction between "to" and "by" by distinguishing the "labeling" role of concepts from the "describing" role of concepts and claiming that the latter ("by") yields "a new level of cognitive achievement." He then asked, "At what age . . . do human children learn to do so?" This is the question I have attempted to answer by saying we ascribe understanding to them even if they themselves cannot ascribe understanding to anyone. And they learn to make such ascriptions when they acquire the concept in the early school years.

ASCRIPTIVISM AND THE COGNITIVE SCIENCE OF UNDERSTANDING

Davidson (2001, p. 74; pp. 205–220) adopted Wittgenstein's suggestion that notions such as understanding, reading, and thinking be approached not as mental states or processes but as ascriptive ones, sorting out the conditions under which understanding, for example, could be appropriately attributed to someone or something. Seeing concepts as word meanings is a bold attempt to move from the somewhat mushy subjective notion of concept to public, observable *sense* of a term, a move to objectivity more commonly attributed to Turing. My initial response to Wittgenstein's proposal was similar to

Bruner's response to AI, namely there goes cognitive psychology down the drain. Hoping to redeem the study of mental processes, I began with the subjective feelings presumably shared by all living creatures and tried to show how feelings became concepts. But in the process, it became clear that what children were acquiring was precisely what some philosophers in the analytic tradition had already worked out, namely that concepts were better seen as word meanings, that beliefs were true or false, the understanding presumed truth and that development was in large part mastering the constraints already laid out in a socially shared natural language.

Davidson (2001, p. 209) claimed that he addressed three problems: how does one know anything about the world, how does one know another's mind, and "how is it possible to know the contents of our own mind without resorting to observation or evidence." He shows that these questions are interdependent, namely one can know about the world only because it is shared with others, that is, objectivity depends on intersubjectivity. He showed that we understand other minds because the language in which that knowledge is represented is a public language; there is no private language, as Wittgenstein had argued. Consequently, concepts apply equally to self and other. Third, we know the contents of our own mind because contents are already experienced subjective states. This third point requires further comment.

I earlier criticized both Janack and Bruner for attributing beliefs and conscious mental states to preverbal children. Conscious mental states become possible through learning a language for ascription and avowal. Introspection is an acquired ability, dependent on language. One learns the concept not by an interior gaze but by learning to use a term in a public language. Montgomery (2005) has argued that the content of a feeling state cannot provide an ostensive definition for a term. The knowledge of the word, not the feeling state, permits the ascription of those states to oneself as introspection. On this alter I sacrificed my earlier cherished assumption, namely that children's early concepts were nonlinguistic mental codes. What codes there are, I now argue, are linguistic codes.

Davidson acknowledges that the linguistic account of mental states seems to deny the givenness of subjective experience. In my view, the immediacy and urgency of subjective experience is the response of the emotional system that anticipates and responds in terms of prior experience. Knowing what we experience depends on language. Humans experience complex emotions, many of which we share with animals. Only concepts in a language allow us to introspect on those feelings. Thus, immediate experience is something we can talk about, but such feelings relate to the reference, not the meaning of the concept.

One further quibble I have with Davidson is his view that beliefs cause actions rather than represent one aspect of the feeling states that do. Action, on my view, is the product of the feeling states of which cognitive content is only one part. Recall the definition of an emotion as having a content conferred by an appraisal of a situation, a predisposition for action, and a feeling tone. Language is important in turning such feeling states into things that can be judged true or false, thought about, planned for, and shared with others, but the causes of action reside in our wishes and goals.

It is a fair question to ask if my analysis of understanding is anything more than a retail version of some aspects of Davidson's account. I would not be disappointed if it were. But I think my account of first-person subjective feelings gives proper place to what Janack called "experience." Subjective experience already includes much of what is needed for a successful behavior except those features intrinsic to language, namely predication, truth, and intersubjectivity. While language thereby grants access to subjective experience, it does not replace those basic experiential commitments embodied in feelings but broadens them and articulates the relationship amongst them. Davidson thinks of subjective experience as a kind of knowledge, whereas I think of it as a kind of emotion with a nonconceptual content, that is, as awareness rather than knowledge. That allowed me to explain the behavior of pre-linguistic children as well as the ways that emotion continues to affect thinking in adult humans.

Where, in my view, I go beyond Davidson's, ascriptivism is the distinction between "ascribe to" and "ascribe by," a distinction that highlights the importance of actually making the ascription and judging that the ascription is appropriate. In this way I bring back some of the issues of agency, intentionality, and responsibility into an account of mental life. However, my claims for originality may not be warranted. Derry (2013, p. 2), in commenting on the work of McDowell and Brandom, wrote: "[T]he gist of the argument is that in order to make a claim of knowing we are not, as commonly thought, giving a description of an event but placing our claims about it in a *space of reasons.*" Precisely! To ascribe understanding to anyone, including the self, is to make a claim, an assertion that is true or false and for which one will be held accountable and for which one must be prepared to offer reasons and evidence to justify the ascriptions. This is what makes understanding a rational process rather than merely a computational one.

What is gained by ascription theory of mind is its demystifica-tion of such diffuse notions as concepts, meanings, and "mental" processes, including "sense-making." Concepts rather than mysteri-ous subjective mental entities become the *senses* of words with rules for their use. This is a step towards both clarity and objectivity, a concern not only to philosophy and psychology but also to a primary concern of the school. But exclusive attention to truth may lead one to overlook the subjective feelings of value, certainty, and relevance of our beliefs, as Proust made clear, as well as the personal identity, agency, intentionality, and responsibility, the loss of which alarmed Janack and Bruner. Better to say, understanding is forming beliefs that are not only true but also seem to be true. Thus, the gains in objectiv-ity that ascriptivism promised is surrendered the moment that ascriptions are recognized as speech acts for which one is responsible and accountable. What is true of mental states in general is true of understanding in particular. Treating understanding as an ascribable concept adds a degree of precision lacking in such notions as making sense.

For Davidson, as I understand him, first-person and third-person ascriptions must meet the same objective standards. Although I have not been able to find him actually saying so, he did write: "Knowledge of our own minds and knowledge of the minds of others are thus mutually dependent" (p. 213). And again, "Third person knowledge – knowledge of other minds – is thus essential to all other knowledge" (p. xvii). For Davidson, this is the source of objectivity, a meeting of minds over a shared referent object. For Davidson, objectivity is just intersubjectivity.

It is important to note that Davidson's logical conclusion is identical to the evidence-based conclusion drawn from research on children's theory of mind. Davidson's first-person, third-person equivalence implies that children will attribute false belief to others only when they are able to ascribe such beliefs to themselves as well. Gopnik and Astington (1988) provided experimental evidence for this first- and third-person equivalence. The children who succeeded in attributing false beliefs to another also succeeded in attributing false beliefs to their own earlier mistakes. The children's achievement was attributed to their acquisition of a concept of belief. These are not conflicting views but rather a demonstration that the concepts of "believing" and "understanding" are acquired and that such concepts depend on a shared public language. The lexical concepts involved are "believe" and "understand," the concepts that permit ascription.

CONCEPTS AND THE REPRESENTATIONAL THEORY OF MIND

The identity conditions for the use of a word in ascribing understanding are just those that make up the concept of understanding. Those conditions, as I emphasize, center on truth. Only linguistic expressions with a subject and a predicate can be true or false. It is the meaning, the *sense* of the word "understand," that enters into sentences. To know the word is to know how to use it to make correct claims about understanding. Knowing the word is knowing the identity conditions of the use of the word "understand" or its equivalents. Those identity conditions are the semantic features, the Fregean *sense*, of the word. Words, unlike feelings, distinguish sense from reference.

To turn concepts into word meanings is to overturn a basic assumption of the Representational Theory of Mind (RTM). RTM assumes that the cognitive processes of animals and nonverbal children are composed of concepts in a private language, sometimes called mentalese. In my view, the RTM is challenged if not refuted by Wittgenstein's "private language argument." Specifically, concepts are the components of beliefs that are true or false. And to be true or false is not a private truth but a social one, made possible by a shared language. The representation mind is a linguistic mind.

Introspection is self-ascription that may be true or false and not just a subjective feeling. Self-ascriptions like other ascriptions are formulated in a public language. Thus, both first- and third-person ascription of a state by means of the word "understand" must meet the same standards, the same "identity conditions," including truth or correctness. Words carry these standards as part of their meaning; feelings do not. Yet, as mentioned earlier, the feeling of understanding may be all that a learner has to go on even when learning the language. Feelings may be referred to but they do not constitute the sense.

Davidson (2001, p. 128) wrote:

> It is not that we have a clear idea what sort of language we could use to describe half-formed minds; there may be a very deep conceptual difficulty or impossibility involved. That means there is a perhaps

insuperable problem in giving a full description of the emergence of thought.

The concept of feeling states with their nonconceptual content and that allow one to go on, I have suggested, may provide the alternative that Davidson sought. Feelings are complex states that are evoked in the present when events confirm or violate the anticipations and predictions of the subject. But it is the acquisition of a natural language with verbal concepts with a sense and a reference that makes thought and reason possible. So it is not feeling that makes thought possible but learning a language.

Whereas feelings involve attunements, predictions, and anticipations, as well as predispositions for action and a phenomenal tone, beliefs are ascribed on the basis of their truth or falsity. We adults are free to ascribe beliefs to sapient creatures if we choose, but we must acknowledge that those creatures, lacking a shared language, cannot ascribe them. So their experience is distinctive from our own; we know our beliefs are possibly false. Beliefs, along with our feelings, are what we, sapient creatures, live by.

The account of understanding I have advanced is thoroughly commonsensical; it appeals only to usage in a public language rather than to hypothetical mental abilities and unconscious brain processes. Davidson wrote that "there seems to be no chance of 'scientific' explanations in this area" (p. 62), suggesting that the computational and brain processes involved in meeting these identity conditions are not part of what we mean by understanding. My only correction is to say that although the identity conditions for understanding make no reference to feeling, for the experiencer there is a feeling of sincerity, satisfaction, and a degree of commitment that accompanies correct understanding. Again, there is something it feels like to understand.

What it means to understand is to know the criteria for correctly ascribing understanding to oneself or others. These criteria, truth and intersubjectivity, are articulated in the various speech and textual communities that one is a participant in. Sorting them out is an important part of conceptual development. These criteria are refined through discourse, through reading, and through being taught. But it is in learning to ascribe understanding to oneself and others that one becomes a rational member of a speech community.

Now I understand.

References

Amsterdam, J. G. & Bruner, J. S. (2000). *Minding the law: How courts rely on storytelling*. Cambridge, MA: Harvard University Press.

Anton, C. (2017). Alphabetic print-based literacy, hermeneutic sociality, and philosophic culture. *Review of Communication, 17*, 257–272.

Apperly, I. A. (2008). Beyond simulation-theory and theory-theory: Why social cognitive neuroscience should use its own concepts to study "theory of mind." *Cognition, 107*, 266–283.

Arendt, H. (1954). *The crisis in education: Between past and future*. New York: Viking.

Astington, J. & Gopnik, A. (1988). Knowing you have changed your mind: Children's understanding of representational change. In J. Astington, P. Harris, & D. R. Olson (Eds.), *Developing theories of mind*. Cambridge, UK: Cambridge University Press.

Astington, J. W. (1996). What is theoretical about the child's theory of mind? A Vygotskian view of its development. In P. Carruthers & P. K. Smith (Eds.), *Theories of theories of mind*. Cambridge, UK: Cambridge University Press.

Astington, J. W. (1998). Theory of mind, Humpty Dumpty, and the icebox. *Human Development, 41*, 30–39.

Astington, J. W., & Baird, J. (2005). *Why language matters for theory of mind*. Oxford: Oxford University Press.

Astington, J. W., Harris, P., & Olson, D. R. (1988). *Developing theories of mind*. Cambridge, UK: Cambridge University Press.

Auerbach, E. (1953). *Mimesis: The representation of reality in Western literature*. Princeton, NJ: Princeton University Press.

Austin, J. L. (1962). *How to do things with words*. Cambridge, MA: Harvard University Press.

Baecker, R. (2019). *Computers in society*. New York: Oxford University Press.

Baillargeon, R. (1986). Representing the existence and the location of hidden objects: Object permanence in 6- and 8-month-old infants. *Cognition, 23*, 21–41.

Bakhurst, D. (2011). *The formation of reason*. Oxford: Wiley-Blackwell.

Baressi, J., & Moore, C. (1996). Intentional relations and social understanding. *Behavioral and Brain Sciences, 19*, 107–154.

Beal, C. (1990). Development of knowledge about the role of inference in text comprehension. *Child Development, 61*, 1011-1023.

Bellugi, U. (1967). The acquisition of the system of negation in children's speech. Unpublished doctoral dissertation. Harvard University.

Bennett, J. (1971). *Locke, Berkeley, Hume: Central themes.* Oxford: Clarendon.

Bereiter, C. & Scardamalia, M. (1987). *The psychology of written composition.* Mahwah, NJ: Erlbaum.

Bereiter, C., & Scardamalia, M. (1993). *Surpassing ourselves: An inquiry into the nature and implications of expertise.* Chicago: Open Court.

Bogden, R. (2009). *Predicative minds: The social ontogeny of propositional thinking.* Cambridge, MA: MIT Press.

Brandom, R. (1994). *Making it explicit: Reasoning, representing and discursive commitment.* Cambridge, MA: Harvard University Press.

Brandom, R. (2009). *Reason in philosophy.* Cambridge, MA: Belknap Press of Harvard University Press.

Brantley, R. E. (1984). *Locke, Wesley, and the method of English Romanticism.* Gainesville: University Press of Florida.

Brentano, R. (1973). *Psychology from an empirical standpoint* (O. Kraus, Ed.). London: RKP. (Original published in 1874.)

Brown, A. (1975). The development of memory: Knowing, knowing about knowing, and knowing how to know. In H. W. Reese (Ed.), *Advances in child development and behavior* (Vol. 10). New York: Academic Press.

Brown, R. (1956). Appendix. In J.S. Bruner, J. Goodnow & G. Austin (Ed.), *A study of thinking.* New York: Wiley.

Bruner, J. S., Goodnow, J., & Austin, G. (1956). *A study of thinking with an appendix by R. Brown.* New York: Wiley.

Bruner, J. S. (1973). *Beyond the information given: Studies in the psychology of knowing* (J. Anglin, Ed.). London: George Allen.

Bruner, J. S. (1983). *Child's talk: Learning to use language.* New York: Norton.

Bruner, J. S. (1990). *Acts of meaning.* Cambridge, MA: Harvard University Press.

Bruner, J. S., Goodnow, J. J., & Austin, G. A. (1956). *A study of thinking* (With an appendix on language by R. W. Brown). New York: Wiley.

Carpenter, P., & Just, M. (1975). Sentence comprehension: A psycholinguistic processing model of verification. *Psychological Review, 82*, 45–73.

Carruthers, P. (1996). *Language, thought and consciousness: An essay in philosophical psychology.* Cambridge: Cambridge University Press.

Chen, X., & Pasquarella, A. (2017). Chinese reading development: The contributions of linguistic and cognitive factors. In L. Verhoeven & C. Perfetti (Eds.),

Learning to read across languages and writing systems. Cambridge: Cambridge University Press.

Chomsky, N. (May 15, 1969). Knowledge of language. *Times Literary Supplement*, p. 523

Clark, A. (2013). Whatever next? Predictive brains, situated agents, and the future of cognitive science. *Behavioral and Brain Sciences, 36*(3), 181–204.

Clark, H. H., & Chase, W. G. (1972). On the process of comparing sentences against pictures. *Cognitive Psychology, 3*, 472–517.

Clark, H. H., & Clark, E. V. (1977). *Psychology and language: An introduction to psycholinguistics*. New York: Harcourt, Brace, Jovanovich.

Coltheart, M., & Coltheart, V. (1997). Reading comprehension is not exclusively reliant upon phonological representation. *Cognitive Neuropsychology, 14*, 167–175.

Damasio, A. (1994). *The feeling of what happens: Body and emotion in the making of consciousness*. New York: Harcourt.

Davidson, D. (2001). *Subjective, intersubjective, objective*. New York: Oxford University Press.

Dennett, D. (1989). *The intentional stance*. Cambridge, MA: MIT Press.

Dennett, D. (1991). *Consciousness explained*. Boston: Little, Brown.

Derry, J. (2013). *Vygotsky philosophy and education*. Oxford: Wiley Blackwell.

Descartes, R. (2004). *Discourse on method* (J. Veitch, Trans.). London: Orion. (Original published in 1637.)

de Waal, F. (1999). Anthromorphism and anthropodeenial: Consistency in our thinking about humans and other animals. *Philosophical Topics, 27*, 255–280.

Dickson, P. (1981). *Children's oral communication skills*. New York: Academic Press.

diSessa, A. (1985). Learning about knowing. *New Directions for Cognitive Development, 28*, 997–1024.

Dummett, M. (1993). *Frege: Philosophy of language* (3rd ed.). Cambridge, MA: Harvard University Press.

Easterly, W. (October 8, 2009). The anarchy of success. *New York Review of Books, 56*, 28–30.

Egan, K. (1997). *The educated mind. How cognitive tools shape our understanding*. Chicago: University of Chicago Press.

Egner, T., Monti, J. M., & Summerfield, C. (2010). Expectation and surprise determine neural population responses in the ventral visual stream. *Journal of Neuroscience, 30*(49), 16601–16608.

Ehri, L. & Wilce, L. (1980). The influence of orthography on reader's conceptualization of the phonemic structure of words. *Applied Psycholinguistics, 1*, 371–385.

Engleman, D. (2011). *Incognito: The secret lives of the brain*. New York: Vintage.

Erneling, C. (2010). *Towards a discursive education*. Cambridge: Cambridge University Press.

Feldman, C. (1987). Thought from language: The linguistic construction of cognitive representations. In J. S. Bruner & H. Haste (Eds.), *Making sense: The child's construction of the world*. London: Methuen.

Ferreiro, E. & Teberosky, A. (1982). *Literacy before schooling*. New York: Heinemann.

Flavell, J. H. (1981). Cognitive monitoring. In W. P. Dickson (Ed.), *Children's oral communication skills*. (pp. 35–60) New York: Academic Press.

Flavell, J. H., Flavell, E. R., & Green, F. L. (1983). Development of the appearance-reality distinction. *Cognitive Psychology, 15*, 95–120.

Fodor, J. (1972). Some reflections on L. S. Vygotsky's Language and Thought. *Cognitive Psychology, 1*, 83–95.

Fodor, J. (1975). *The language of thought*. New York: Thomas Crowell.

Francis, N. (2019). Literacy and the language awareness hypothesis. *Writing Systems Research, 11*(2), 176–187.

Gadamer, H.-G. (1975). *Truth and method*. London: Sheed & Ward.

Gleitman, L. (1986). Biological dispositions to learn language. In W. Demopoulos & A. Marras (Eds.), *Language learning and concept acquisition: Foundational Issues*. Norwood: Ablex.

Gleitman, Lila R. (1990). The structural source of verb meaning. *Language Acquisition, 1* (1): 3–55.

Gilbert, D. T. (1991). How mental systems believe. *American Psychologist, 46*, 107–119.

Goldman, S. (2006). *Simulating minds: The philosophy, psychology and neuroscience of mindreading*. New York: Oxford University Press.

Goldman, A., & Shanton, K. (2010). Simulation theory. *Wiley Interdisciplinary Review: Cognitive Science, 1*(4), 527–538.

Goody, E. N. (1978). Towards a theory of questions. In E. N. Goody (Ed.), *Questions and politeness*. Cambridge: Cambridge University Press.

Gopnik, A., & Astington, J. (1988). Children's understanding of representational change and it relation to the understanding of false belief and the appearance-reality distinction. *Child Development, 59*, 26–37.

Gopnik, A., & Meltzoff, A. (1997). *Words, thoughts, and theories*. Cambridge, MA: Bradford/Harvard University Press.

Gough, P. B., Hoover, W. A., & Peterson, C. L. (1996). Some observation on a simple view of reading. In C. Cornoldi & J. Oakhill (Eds.), *Reading comprehension difficulties: Processes and intervention*. Mahwah, NJ: Erlbaum.

Green, M. (1996). A rereading of Dewey's art as experience. In D. R. Olson & N. G. Torrance (Eds.), *The Handbook of education and human development*. Oxford: Blackwell.

Grice, H. P. (1989). *Studies in ways with words*. Cambridge, MA: Harvard University Press.

Griffin, S. (1988). *Children's awareness of their inner world*. Unpublished PhD thesis, OISE/University of Toronto.

Hacking, I. (1996). Normal people. In D. R. Olson & N. Torrance (Eds.), *Modes of thought*. Cambridge: Cambridge University Press.

Harris, P. L. (2020). The point, the shrug, and the question of clarification. In L. P. Butler, S. Ronfard, and K. H. Corriveau (Eds.), *The questioning child: Insights from psychology and education*. Cambridge, UK: Cambridge University Press.

Herbart, J. (1898). *The application of psychology to the science of education*. New York: Scribner.

Heath, J. (2011). *Following the rules: Practical reasoning and the deontic constraint*. Oxford: Oxford University Press.

Hinton, G. (2007). Learning multiple layers of representation. *Trends in Cognitive Science, 11*, 428–434.

Hinton, G. (2014). Where do features come from? *Cognitive Science, 38*(6), 1078–1101.

Hume, D. (1993). *Enquiries concerning human understanding* (E. Steinberg, Ed.). Indianapolis: Hackett.

Huttenlocher, J. (1964). Children's language: Word-phrase relationships. *Science, 143*, 264–265.

Illich, I. (1991). A plea for research on lay literacy. In D. Olson & N. Torrance (Eds.), *Literacy and orality*. Cambridge: Cambridge University Press.

Jackendoff, R. (2002). *Foundations of language*. Oxford: Oxford University Press.

Jackendoff, R. (2012). *A users guide to thought and meaning*. New York: Oxford University Press.

Jacob, P. (1997). *What minds can do: Intentionality in a non-intentional world*. Cambridge: Cambridge University Press.

James, W. (1890/2007). *The principles of psychology*. Vol. 1. New York: Cosimo Classics.

Janack, M. (2012). *What we mean by experience*. Stanford: Stanford University Press.

Johnson, C. (1988). Theories of mind and the structure of conscious experience. In J. Astington, P. Harris, & D. R. Olson (Eds.), *Developing theories of mind*. Cambridge: Cambridge University Press.

Johnson, C. N., & Maratsos, M. P. (1977). Early comprehensions of mental verbs: Think and know. *Child Development, 48,* 1743–1747.

Kahneman, D. (2011). *Thinking fast and slow.* Toronto, ON: Penguin.

Karmiloff-Smith, A. (1992). *Beyond modularity: A developmental perspective on cognitive science.* Cambridge, MA: MIT Press.

Katz, J., & Fodor, J. (1963). The structure of semantic theory. *Language, 39,* 170–210.

Kendler, T., & Kendler, H. (1959). Reversal and nonreversal shifts in kindergarten children. *Journal of Experimental Psychology, 58,* 56–60.

Kintsch, W. (1998). *Comprehension: A paradigm for cognition.* Cambridge: Cambridge University Press.

Kiparsky, P., & Kiparsky, C. (1970). Fact. In M. Bierwisch & K. Heidolph (Eds.), *Progress in linguistics.* The Hague: Mouton.

Korzybski, A. (1933). *Science and sanity.* Lakeville: The International Non-Aristotelian Library Publishing Company.

Kramer, S. (2012). The 'eye of the mind' and the eye of the body; Descartes and Leibniz on truth, mathematics and visuality. In F. G. Barth, P. G. Deutsch, & H. D. Klein (Eds.), *Sensory perception: Mind and matter* (pp. 369–382). Wien, Austria: Springer.

Kuperberg, G. R., & Jaeger, T. F. (2016). What do we mean by prediction in language comprehension? *Language and Cognitive Neuroscience, 31,* 32–59.

Lagemann, E. C. (2000). *The elusive science: The troubling history of educational research.* Chicago: University of Chicago Press.

Lazarus, R. S. (1999). The cognition-emotion debate: A bit of history. In T. Dalgleish & M. Power (Eds.), *Handbook of cognition and emotion.*

Lee, E. (1995). Young children's representational understanding of intention. Unpublished PhD, OISE, University of Toronto.

Lee, C., White, G., & Dong, D. (Eds.). (2021). Executive Summary. Educating for Civic Reasoning and Discourse. Committee on Civic Reasoning and Discourse. Washington: National Academy of Education.

Lee, E., Torrance, N., & Olson, D. R. (2001). Young children and the say/mean distinction: Verbatim and paraphrase recognition in narrative and nursery rhyme contexts. *Journal of Child Language, 28,* 531–543.

Lemann, N. (2020). Can Journalism be saved? *New York Review of Books,* LXVII, February 27, 2020.

Lepore, J. (2020). The isolation ward: On loneliness. *The New Yorker,* April 6, 2020, 62–64.

Leslie, A. M. (1987). Pretense and representation: The origins of "theory of mind". *Psychological Review, 94,* 412–429.

Levesque, H. (2017). *Common sense, the Turing Test and the quest for real AI.* Cambridge, MA: MIT Press.

Levine, T. (2019). *Duped: Truth-default theory and the social science of lying and deception.* Tuscaloosa: University of Alabama Press.

Lewis, M. (2014). *The rise of consciousness and the development of emotional life.* New York: Guilford Press.

Liublinskaya, A. A. (1957). The development of children's speech and thought. In B. Simon (Ed.), *Psychology in the Soviet Union.* Stanford: Stanford University Press.

Locke, J. (1829), *An essay concerning human understanding.* London: Thomas Tegg. (Originally published in 1689).

Lockl, K., & Schneider, W. (2016). Precursors of metamemory in young children: The role of theory of mind and metacognition vocabulary. *Metacognition Learning, 1,* 15–31.

MacDonald, P. (2012). *Languages of intentionality.* New York: Continuum.

Macnamara, J. (1986). *A border dispute: The place of logic in psychology.* Cambridge: Cambridge University Press.

Malinowski, B. (1923). The problem of meaning in primitive languages. In C. K. Ogden & I. A. Richards (Eds.), *The meaning of meaning (Supplementary essays).* New York: Harcourt Brace.

Malvestuto-Filice, G. R. (1986). The development of the understanding of the intentional predicates "pretend" and "imagine". Unpublished doctoral dissertation. University of Toronto.

Markman, E. M. (1976). Children's difficulty with the word-referent differentiation. *Child Development, 47,* 742–749.

Markman, E. M. (1977). Realizing you don't understand: A preliminary investigation. *Child Development, 48,* 986–992.

Markman, E. M. (1981). Comprehension monitoring. In W. P. Dickson (Ed.), *Children's oral communication skills.* (pp. 61–82). New York: Academic Press.

McDougall, W. (1911). *Body and mind.* London: Methuen.

McDowell, J. (1994). *Mind and world.* Cambridge, MA: Harvard University Press.

McGinn, C. (1991). *The problem of consciousness.* Oxford: Blackwell.

Miller, C. (2018). *The death of the gods: A new global power grab.* Portsmouth: Heinemann.

Miller, G. (1979). Images, models, similes and metaphors. In A. Ortony (Ed.), *Metaphor and thought.* Cambridge: Cambridge University Press.

Misak, S. (2013). *The American Pragmatists.* Oxford: Oxford University Press.

Montgomery, D. E. (2005). The developmental origins of meaning for mental terms. In J. W. Astington & J. Baird (Eds.), *Why language matters for theory of mind.* Oxford: Oxford University Press.

Morrison, K. F. (1990). *History as a visual art in the Twelfth-Century Renaissance.* Princeton: Princeton University Press.

Nagel, T. (1974). What is it like to be a bat? *Philosophical Review, 83,* 435–450.

Nagy, W. E., Herman, P. A., & Anderson, R. C. (1985). Learning words from context. *Reading Research Quarterly, 20*(2), 233–253.

National Centre for Educational Statistics (2010). *The nation's report card: Graade 12 reading and mathematics 2009 national and pilot state results (NCES 2011-455).* Washington, DC: Institute of Educational Sciences, US Department of Education.

Nelson, K. (2005). Language pathways into the community of minds. In J. W. Astington & J. A. Baird (Eds.), *Why language matters for theory of mind.* Oxford: Oxford University Press.

Nussbaum, M. (2001). *Upheavals of thought: The intelligence of emotions.* Cambridge: Cambridge University Press.

Oatley, K. (1992) *Best laid schemes: The psychology of emotions.* Cambridge: Cambridge University Press.

Oatley, K., & Johnson-Laird, P. (1996). The communicative theory of emotions. In L. Martin & A. Tesser (Eds.), *Striving and feeling: Interactions among goals, affect and self-regulation.* Mahwah: Erlbaum.

Olson, D. R. (1970). Language and thought: Aspects of a cognitive theory of semantics. *Psychological Review, 77*(4), 257–273.

Olson, D. R. (1975). Review of J. B. Carroll & J. Chall *"Toward a literate society". Proceedings of the National Academy of Education,* (Vol. 2, pp. 109–178). Stanford: National Academy of Education.

Olson, D. R. (1977). From utterance to text: The bias of language in speech and writing. *Harvard Educational Review, 47,* 257–281.

Olson, D. R. (1989). Making up your mind: Presidential address to the Canadian Psychological Association. *Canadian Psychology, 30,* 17–27.

Olson, D. R. (1994). *The world on paper.* Cambridge, UK: Cambridge University Press.

Olson, D. R. (2003). *Psychological theory and educational reform: How school remakes mind and society.* Cambridge, UK: Cambridge University Press.

Olson, D. R. (2007). The self-ascription of intention: Responsibility, obligation and self-control. *Synthese, 159,* 297–314.

Olson, D. R. (2016). *The mind on paper: Reading, consciousness and rationality.* Cambridge: Cambridge University Press.

Olson, D. R., & Astington, J. W. (1986). Children's acquisition of metalinguistic and metacognitive verbs. In W. Demopoulos & A. Marras (Eds.), *Language learning and concept acquisition.* Norwood: Ablex.

Olson, D. R., & Astington, J. W. (2013). Preschool children conflate pragmatic agreement and semantic truth. *First Language, 33,* 617–627.

Olson, D. R., & Bruner, J. S. (1996). Folk psychology and folk pedagogy. In D. R. Olson & N. G. Torrance (Eds.), *The handbook of education and human development*. Oxford: Blackwell.

Olson, D. R., & Campbell, R. (1993). Constructing representations. In C. Pratt & A. F. Garton (Eds.), *Systems of representation in children: Development and use* (pp. 11–26). Chichester: Wiley.

Olson, D. R., & Filby, N. (1972). On the comprehension of active and passive sentences. *Cognitive Psychology, 3*(3), 361–381.

Olson, D. R., & Kamawar, D. (2002). Writing as a form of quotation. In J. Brockmeier, M. Wang & D. R. Olson (Eds.), *Literacy, narrative and culture*. Richmond: Curzon Press.

Olson, D. R., & Oatley, K. (2014). The quotation theory of writing. *Written Communication, 31*, 4–26.

Ong, W. (1982). *Orality and literacy: The technologizing of the word*. London: Methuen.

Papafragou, A. & Musolino, J. (2003). Scalar implicatures: Experiments at the semantic-pragmatic interface. *Cognition, 86*, 253-282.

Pea, R. (1980). The development of negation in early childhood. In D. R. Olson (Ed.), *The social foundations of language and thought: Essays in honor of Jerome S. Bruner*. New York: Norton.

Pearson, P. D. (2014). The reading wars. *Educational Policy, 18*, 216–222.

Pearson, P. D., Palincsar, A. S., Biancarosa, G., & Berman, A. (Eds.) (2020). *Reaping the rewards of the reading for understanding initiative*. Washington: National Academy of Education.

Perner, J. (1991). *Understanding the representational mind*. Cambridge, MA: MIT Press.

Peskin, J., & Astington, J. W. (2004). The effects of adding metacognitive language to story texts. *Cognitive Development, 19*, 253–273.

Piaget, J. (1962). *Play, dreams and imitation in childhood*. New York: Norton.

Pinker, S. (1994). *The language instinct*. New York: Harper Collins.

Popper, K. (1972). *Objective knowledge: An evolutionary approach*. Oxford: Oxford University Press.

Premack, D., & Woodruff, G. (1978). Does the chimpanzee have a theory of mind. *Behavioral and Brain Sciences, 1*, 515–526.

Proust, J. (2014). *The philosophy of metacognition: Mental agency and self-awareness*. Oxford: Oxford University Press.

Pylyshyn, Z. (1984). *Computation and cognition: Toward a foundation for cognitive science*. Cambridge, MA: MIT Press.

Quine, W. (1960). *Word and object*. Cambridge, MA: MIT Press.

Ravitch, D. (2011). *The death and life of the American school system: How testing and choice are undermining education.* New York: Basic Books.

Ravitch, D. (2021). *The dark history of school choice.* New York: New York Review of Books, LXVIII, 36–38.

Ricoeur, P. (1981). *Hermeneutics & the human sciences.* (J. B. Thompson, Trans.). Cambridge: Cambridge University Press.

Robinson, E., Goelman, H., & Olson, D. R. (1983). Children's understanding of the relationship between expressions (what is said) and intentions (what is meant). *British Journal of Developmental Psychology, 1*, 75–86.

Rorty, R. (1981). *Philosophy and the mirror of nature.* Princeton, NJ: Princeton University Press.

Rozeboom, W. (1972). Problems in the psycho-philosophy of knowledge. In J. Royce & W. Rozeboom (Eds.), *The psychology of knowing.* New York: Gordon and Breach.

Russell, R. (1948). *Human knowledge: Its scope and limitations.* London: Allen & Unwin.

Ryle, G. (2009). *The concept of mind.* London: Routledge.

Saussure, F. de (1958). *Course in general linguistics* (W. Baskin, Trans.). London: Duckworth. (Original published in 1916).

Schachter, S. & Singer, J. (1962). Cognitive, Social, and Physiological Determinants of Emotional State (PDF). *Psychological Review, 69*(5), 379–399. doi:10.1037/h0046234.

Scherer, K., & Moors, A. (2019). The emotion process: Event appraisal and component differentiation. *Annual Review of Psychology, 70*, 719–745.

Schneider, W. (2008). The development of metacognitive knowledge in children and adolescents: Major implications for education. *Mind, Brain and Education, 2*, 114–121.

Seabrook, J. (2019). The next word: Where will predictive text take us? *The New Yorker*, October 14, p. 63.

Searle, J. (1983). *Intentionality: An essay in the philosophy of mind.* Cambridge: Cambridge University Press.

Seidenberg, M. (2017). *Language at the speed of sight.* New York: Basic Books.

Sellars, W. (1997). *Empiricism and the philosophy of mind.* Introduction by R. Rorty and study guide by R. Brandom. Cambridge, MA: Harvard University Press. (Originally published in 1956).

Share, D. (2014). Alphabetism in reading science. *Frontiers in Psychology, 5*, 512.

Sliwa, P. (2015). Understanding and knowing. *Proceedings of the Aristotlian Society, CXV, Part I.*

Slobin, D. I. (2003). Language and thought online: Cognitive consequences of linguistic relativity. In D. Gentner & S. Goldin-Meadow (Eds.), *Language in mind: Advances in the investigation of language and thought* (pp. 157–191). Cambridge, MA: MIT Press.

Sloman, S. A. (1996). The empirical case for two systems of reasoning. *Psychological Bulletin, 119*, 3–22.

Smith, E. E., Shoben, E. J., & Rips, L. J. (1974). Structure and process in semantic memory: A featural model for semantic decisions. *Psychological Review, 1*, 214–241.

Smith, F. (1971). *Understanding reading.* Portsmouth: Heinemann.

Spinoza, B. (1677/1901). *Improvement of the understanding, ethics and correspondence.* Washington: Walter Dunne, Publisher.

Stanford Encyclopedia of Philosophy. (2006). *The Turing Test.*

Stanovich, K. (1999). *Who is rational? Studies of individual differences in reasoning.* Mahwah, NJ: Erlbaum.

Stanovich, K. (2009). *What intelligence tests miss: The psychology of rational thought.* New Haven, CT: Yale University Press.

Stock, B. (1983). *The implications of literacy.* Princeton: Princeton University Press.

Strawson, G. (2008). *Real materialism and other essays.* Oxford: Clarendon.

Sun, J., Anderson, R. C., Morris, J. A., Lin, T.-J., Miller, B. W., Ma, S., Kim, T., & Scott, T. (2017). Children's engagement and affect during Collaborative Learning and Direct Instruction. (Unpublished).

Sutscover, I. (2019). Interview. *The New Yorker*, October 14. (See Seebrook, 2019).

Taylor, C. (2016). *The language animal: The full shape of the human linguistic capacity.* Cambridge, MA: Belknap/Harvard University Press.

Tomasello, M. (2019). *Becoming human: A theory of ontogeny.* Cambridge, MA: Belknap Press.

Torrance, N. G., & Olson, D. R. (1987). Development of the metalanguage and the acquisition of literacy. *Interchange, 18*, 136–146.

Tunmer, W. E., & Herriman, M. L. (1984). The development of metalinguistic awareness: A conceptual overview. In W. E. Tunmer, C. Pratt, & M. L. Herriman (Eds.), *Metalinguistic awareness in children; theory, research, and implications.* Berlin: Springer-Verlag.

Turing, A. (1950). Computing machinery and intelligence. *Mind, 59*(236), 433–460. (p. 442).

Turing Test. (2006). *Stanford Encyclopedia of Philosophy.* (Wikipedia).

Turner, N., & Thomas, F.-N. (2011). *Clear and simple as the truth: Writing about prose.* Princeton: Princeton University Press.

de Villiers, J. G. (2005). Can language acquisition give children a point of view? In J. W. Astington & J. Baird (Eds.), *Why language matters for theory of mind*. Oxford: Oxford University Press.

de Villiers, J. G., & Pyers, J. (2002). Complements to cognition: A longitudinal study of the relationship between complex syntax and false-belief understanding. *Cognitive Development, 17*, 1037–1060.

Vygotsky, L. S. (1986). *Thought and language* (A. Kozulin, Ed.). Cambridge, MA: Harvard University Press.

Wason, P. (1980). The verification task and beyond. In D. R. Olson (Ed.), *The social foundations of language and thought*. New York: Norton.

Weir, R. (1962). *Language in the crib*. Madison: University of Wisconsin.

Welllman, H. M., Cross, D., & Watson, J. (2001). Meta-analysis of theory of mind development: The truth about false belief. *Child Development, 72*, 655–684.

Wertsch, J. (2000). Vygotsky's two minds on the nature of meaning. In W. Bechtel & G. Graham (Eds.), *Vygotskian perspectives on literacy research*. Cambridge, UK: Cambridge University Press.

Wimmer, H., & Perner, J. (1983). Beliefs about beliefs: Representation and constraining function of wrong beliefs in young children's understanding of deception. *Cognition, 13*, 103–128.

Wimmer, H., Hogrefe, J., & Sodian, B. (1988). A second stage in children's conception of mental life: Understanding informational accesses as origins of knowledge and belief. In J. Astington, P. Harris, & D. R. Olson (Eds.), *Developing theories of mind*. Cambridge: Cambridge University Press.

Winner, E. (1988). *The point of words: Children's understanding of metaphor and irony*. Cambridge, MA: Harvard University Press.

Wittgenstein, L. (1953). *Philosophical investigations*. Oxford: Blackwell.

Wolf, M. (2018). *Reader, come home: The reading brain in a digital world*. New York: HarperCollins.

Zelazo, P., & Jacques, S. (1996). Children's rules use: Representation, reflection and cognitive control. *Annals of Child Development, 12*, 119–176.

Zimmerman, B. J. (1990). Self-regulated learning and academic achievement: An overview. *Educational Psychologist, 25*(1), 3–17.

Index

Milton Keynes UK
Ingram Content Group UK Ltd.
UKHW020627081223
434004UK00008B/76